I LOVE DINNER COOKBOOK

Easy Dinner Recipes That Will Make You Love Dinner Again

Katie Moseman

First Edition

Text and Photographs © 2019 Katie Moseman

All rights reserved. No part of this book may be reproduced by any means whatsoever without written permission from the publisher, except brief portions quoted for purpose of review.

Cover by Katie Moseman

Interior by Ashley Ruggirello at www.CardboardMonet.com

*For my mom,
who sometimes calls it supper.*

ALSO BY KATIE MOSEMAN

I Hate Vegetables Cookbook: Fresh and Easy Vegetable Recipes That Will Change Your Mind

Gluten Free World Tour: Internationally Inspired Gluten Free Recipes

Fixin' to Eat: Southern Cooking for the Southern at Heart

Table of Contents

Introduction i

Beef 1
- Red Wine Pot Roast 2
- Bacon and Blue Cheese Pasta with Grilled Steak 3
- Meatza 4
- Tater Tot Hotdish 5
- Steak and Egg Bowl 6
- Vietnamese Banh Mi Bowls 7
- Baked Cavatini 8
- Greek Meatball Salad 10
- New York Strip Roast 11
- Bison Meatloaf 13
- Quick Spaghetti and Meatballs 14
- Chili Cheese Potato Parfait 15
- Smash Burgers 16
- Boliche (Cuban Stuffed Roast) 17

Pork 21
- One Pan Roasted Asian Pork and Vegetables 22
- Pork Chops and Sauerkraut 23
- Gnocchi with Italian Sausage 25
- Pulled Pork in the Oven 26
- Roast Pork Loin Filet with Whole Mushrooms 27
- Irish Bacon and Cheese Frittata 28
- Corn and Andouille Sausage Chowder 30
- Sherry Apple Pork Roast 31

Poultry 33
- Mushroom and Swiss Stuffed Turkey Burgers 34
- Yogurt Marinated Chicken 35
- Buffalo Chicken Quesadillas 36
- Apple Cranberry Pecan Chicken Salad 37
- Spinach Cream Cheese Stuffed Chicken Breasts Wrapped in Bacon 38
- Turkey Reuben Panini 39
- Grilled Chicken Caesar Salad 40
- Tortilla Chip Crusted Turkey Cutlets 41

Seafood 43
- Cedar Plank Salmon 44
- Amalfi Coast Risotto 45
- Citrus Chimichurri Shrimp Rice 46
- Thai Shrimp Curry 49
- Tuna Cakes 50
- Basil Buttered Shrimp with Vegetables 52
- Spicy Shrimp Tacos 53
- Latkes with Smoked Salmon 55
- Tuna Salad Wraps 56
- Salmon with Dill Honey Mustard Sauce 57
- Lemon Pepper Cod 58

Vegetarian 61
- Black Rice with Butternut Squash 62
- Rigatoni with Arugula Pistou 63
- Sheet Pan Tahini Roasted Vegetables 64
- Broccoli Cheese Soup 66
- Toasty Bagel Sandwiches 67
- Cilantro Pesto Black Bean Burgers 68
- Tarragon Goat Cheese Egg Salad Sandwiches 69
- Creamy Potato Soup 70
- Grilled Pimento Cheese Sandwiches 71

On the Side 73
- Roasted Vegetables 75
- Baked Potatoes 76
- Salad 77

Recipe Index 78
Know Your Ingredients Index 79
Contributors 80
Recommended Reading 82
About the Author 83

Introduction

Why is this book called I Love Dinner Cookbook?

When I first started writing this cookbook, the title was purely aspirational. I didn't love dinner, but I wanted to love dinner. I wanted to feel like dinner could be fun, not like dinner was an 800 pound gorilla waiting to pummel me at the end of a long day. So I began testing dinner recipes one by one. Only recipes that made me love dinner again made it into the final cookbook. These are my favorites, the ones I returned to again and again with a smile on my face. I love dinner, and I think you can love dinner, too!

How is this cookbook different?

In this cookbook, it's always dinnertime. Feel like a comfort food dinner? Try Tater Tot Hotdish. Looking for something light and quick? Flip to Lemon Pepper Cod. There are dinners in every style, from indulgent to health-conscious, made with a wholesome variety of ingredients. There are plenty of vegetarian options, too. Every single recipe can be made gluten free if desired. Everything from familiar classics to modern fresh takes are included in one streamlined cookbook that's perfect for finding new cooking inspiration.

How is this cookbook organized?

I Love Dinner Cookbook is organized by main ingredient: beef, pork, poultry, seafood, and vegetarian. Helpful sidebars can be found throughout the cookbook. "Know Your Ingredients" shines a spotlight on particular ingredients to help you learn how to use them. In the dinner recipes, ingredients are listed in the order used, and instructions are broken into clear, short steps that are easy to follow. As a bonus, you also get a handy "On the Side" guide to making salads, baked potatoes, and roasted vegetables to pair with a main course.

Beef

Red Wine Pot Roast

Why You'll Love It:
Red wine pot roast looks like the cover of a fancy food magazine, but in truth it's ridiculously simple to make. Pot roast works well as a weekend meal, when you have time to let it cook low and slow.

Prep Time: 15 minutes | Cook Time: 3 hours minimum | Total Time: 3 hours 15 minutes | Yield: 6 to 8 servings

Heat a Dutch oven or large pot over medium heat until hot. Season the roast on all sides with salt and pepper. Place the roast in the pot and sear on each side until the roast is mostly browned on the outside.

Pour in the red wine and broth. Add the carrots, potatoes, and bay leaves. Return to a boil. Cover and reduce heat to low. Simmer for at least 3 hours, but possibly longer. You'll know the roast is done when a gentle tug with a fork causes the roast to fall apart.

Remove the roast and vegetables to a casserole dish, then cover it to keep everything warm and moist. Retrieve the bay leaves and discard.

In a small bowl, whisk cornstarch into 2 tablespoons cold water. Bring the liquid in the pot back to a boil. Add the cornstarch mixture a little at a time, stirring the pot constantly, allowing it to boil for 1 or 2 minutes. The liquid in the pot will thicken into a rich gravy. (Note that it will thicken even more as it cools; don't be tempted to add extra cornstarch mixture, or the gravy will become too thick.)

Taste the gravy and add salt and pepper, if needed, to taste (start with a pinch of each and go from there). Serve portions of roast and vegetables with gravy ladled over the top.

Salt

Pepper

2 pounds boneless chuck roast (approximate weight; does not need to be exact)

2 cups red wine

2 cups beef stock

1 pound carrots, cut into rounds

1 pound baby potatoes

2 bay leaves

2 tablespoons cornstarch

Bacon and Blue Cheese Pasta with Grilled Steak

Why You'll Love It:
Bacon and blue cheese is a classic flavor pairing. Add in slices of strip steak and serve it over pasta, and you have a winning combination that satisfies. If you don't have a grill, you can cook the steak in a grill pan on the stovetop.

Prep Time: 15 minutes | Inactive Time: 45 minutes | Cook Time: 30 minutes
Total Time: 1 hour 30 minutes | Yield: 4 servings

Cook bacon until crispy according to package instructions. Transfer bacon to a paper towel lined plate. Once bacon is cool, cut into bite-sized pieces.

Place steak on a plate or platter. Drizzle 2 teaspoons olive oil on steak and rub to coat both sides. Allow steak to come to room temperature, about 45 minutes.

Heat grill to medium-high heat (about 450°F).

Season steak with 1 teaspoon salt and ½ teaspoon black pepper. Grill steak until desired doneness, about 4 minutes on each side for medium-rare.

Allow steak to rest for 10 minutes after grilling. Thinly slice diagonally and across the grain.

Remove and discard woody ends of asparagus (bend each and it will break where woody end begins).

Drizzle 1 teaspoon olive oil on asparagus. Sprinkle ½ teaspoon salt and ¼ teaspoon black pepper on asparagus.

Grill asparagus until crisp-tender, about 2 or 3 minutes.

Cook pasta according to package instructions. Reserve some of the pasta water to use if needed. Drain pasta.

While pasta is cooking, melt butter in a large saucepan over medium-high heat.

Add flour, stir, and cook for 1 minutes.

Slowly pour in milk, whisking constantly while pouring.

Add remaining 1/4 teaspoon salt and white pepper.

Bring milk mixture to a boil, stirring constantly.

Add 4 ounces blue cheese and continue to cook and stir until cheese is mostly melted (there will be some lumps).

Stir in cooked pasta.

Fold in most of the bacon, steak, and asparagus.

If sauce becomes too thick, stir in a little of the reserved pasta water.

Serve topped with remaining bacon, steak, asparagus, and blue cheese scattered on top.

Special Equipment: Grill or grill pan

3 slices thick-cut bacon

12 ounce strip steak

3 teaspoons olive oil, divided

1 ¾ teaspoons salt, divided

¾ teaspoon fresh ground black pepper, divided

½ pound asparagus

½ pound uncooked penne pasta (gluten free: substitute gluten free penne or similar sized gluten free pasta)

1 tablespoon unsalted butter

1 tablespoon all purpose flour (gluten free: substitute gluten free baking mix flour)

¼ teaspoon ground white pepper

1 cup milk

5 ounces blue cheese crumbles, divided

Meatza

Why You'll Love It:
Meat lovers will be thrilled with this pizza made with a meat base instead of bread. You can customize it by adding your favorite toppings before broiling in the last step.

Prep Time: 10 minutes | Cook Time: 35 minutes | Total Time: 45 minutes | Yield: 3 to 4 servings

Place one oven rack in the middle of the oven, and the other oven rack 6 inches from the broiler element (it's easier than moving an oven rack later, when they're hot). Preheat the oven to bake at 375°F.

In a large mixing bowl, mix together ¼ cup pizza sauce, 1 tablespoon grated parmesan cheese, and Italian seasoning. Add the ground beef and mix until thoroughly combined.

Place the mixture in the center of a deep dish pizza pan (do not use the type of pizza pan that has holes) or a rimmed baking sheet. Pat down the ground beef mixture until it forms a flat circle about 11 inches in diameter.

Place the baking sheet in the oven on the middle rack. Bake for 30 minutes.

Remove the baking sheet from the oven. Turn off the bake function and turn the broiler to high. If there is a great deal of liquid on or around the cooked beef (this will vary by brand and composition of the beef), gently dab it away with a few paper towels so there are no puddles.

Evenly coat the top of the meat with the remaining ½ cup pizza sauce all the way to the very edge of the "crust." Sprinkle on the shredded mozzarella evenly all the way to the edge, then sprinkle the remaining tablespoon of parmesan cheese on top.

Place the baking sheet in the oven on the top rack (the rack 6 inches from the broiler element). Broil time will vary depending on how quickly your broiler element gets hot, and how hot it gets. Start with 2 minutes under the broiler, then increase in 1 minute increments until the cheese is fully melted and dotted with brown spots, which can take up to 5 minutes total. Remove from oven and let cool slightly before serving.

¾ cup pizza sauce, divided

2 tablespoons grated parmesan cheese, divided

1 tablespoon Italian seasoning

1 pound lean ground beef

1 ½ cups shredded low moisture part-skim mozzarella cheese

Tater Tot Hotdish

Why You'll Love It:
Midwestern American comfort food at it best, this casserole or "hotdish" is ideal for fall and winter. It's satisfying and uncomplicated.

Prep Time: 15 minutes | Cook Time: 1 hour 15 minutes | Total Time: 1 hour 30 minutes | Yield: 6 servings

Preheat oven to 350°F. Cook the ground beef into crumbles in a large skillet over medium heat until done, about 10 minutes.

Mix together the cooked ground beef, green beans, and broccoli cheese soup. Spread the mixture into the bottom of a large casserole dish or baking pan.

Sprinkle the shredded cheddar evenly over the mixture. Arrange the tater tots in rows across the top of the cheese layer, leaving a little bit of space between tots so they can get as crispy as possible while cooking.

Bake for 1 hour and 15 minutes, or until the tater tots are crisp and the casserole is brown around the edges and bubbling all over. Let cool for 15 minutes before serving.

1 pound lean ground beef

1 cup broccoli cheese soup (gluten free: substitute gluten free broccoli soup or similar creamy soup)

1 ½ cups cooked green beans

1 ½ cups shredded extra sharp cheddar

4 cups frozen tater tots

Steak and Egg Bowl

Why You'll Love It:
With enough protein to satisfy the most powerful hunger, this steak and egg bowl will make breakfast for dinner your new habit.

Prep Time: 5 minutes | Inactive Time: 1 hour | Cook Time: 15 minutes
Total Time: 1 hour 20 minutes | Yield: 4 servings

For the marinade:

Whisk together the olive oil, Worcestershire sauce, and Dijon mustard. Coat the flank steak all over, cover it, and allow it to marinade for 1 hour, or overnight.

For the steak and egg bowl:

Preheat a nonstick skillet over medium high heat. Once the skillet is hot, place the flank steak in the skillet and cook for 4 minutes, undisturbed and uncovered. Flip the steak and cook for 4 more minutes. Remove the steak and cover loosely to rest.

Remove the pan from the heat and let it cool down while you prepare the eggs.

Beat together the eggs and heavy cream. Once the skillet is cool enough, you can wipe it clean and place it back on the burner, this time over medium-low heat. Heat the pan until hot, then add the butter. It should foam lightly and sizzle very gently.

Pour the beaten eggs into the pan. Cook until a layer of cooked egg forms on the bottom of the pan (about 1 or 2 minutes), then gently push the layer of cooked egg into the center of the pan, allowing the uncooked eggs to run onto the pan surface. Continue to cook for another 2 minutes, gently moving or turning the cooked eggs, until they are no longer liquid.

Divide the scrambled eggs into 4 portions. Slice the cooked steak across the grain evenly into thin slices, then divide the slices into 4 portions. Slice the avocado and divide the slices evenly between the portions. Garnish with salt and pepper to taste (start with a little pinch of each), then serve immediately.

For the marinade:

¼ cup olive oil

2 tablespoons Worcestershire sauce

1 tablespoon Dijon mustard

For the steak and egg bowl:

1 ¾ pounds flank steak

6 large eggs

2 tablespoons heavy cream

2 teaspoons butter

1 avocado

Salt

Pepper

Vietnamese Banh Mi Bowls

Why You'll Love It:
Colorful and flavorful veggies and herbs make every bite of this dinner bowl a new sensation of taste.

Prep Time: 5 minutes | Inactive Time: 30 minutes, or overnight | Cook Time: 15 minutes
Total Time: 50 minutes | Yield: 4 servings

Slice the flank steak into thin strips. Combine all the marinade ingredients (fish sauce, Thai chili, garlic, mint, basil, cilantro) in a large bowl and add the sliced steak. Stir well to coat. Set aside to marinate for 30 minutes or overnight.

In a bowl, combine the radishes, carrots, jalapeño, rice vinegar, and coconut aminos with a pinch of salt and pepper. Toss to coat, then refrigerate until ready to serve.

When the steak is done marinating, bring a cast iron skillet to medium-high heat. In batches, cook the slices of steak until slightly charred on both sides, or until they're about medium-rare.

Fill plates with lettuce, cucumbers, avocado, fresh mint, cilantro, and basil, and top with the cooked steak, then serve with the pickled veggies and a wedge of lime.

Recipe contributed by Caitlin Self (MS, CNS, LDN), the licensed nutritionist behind www.frugalnutrition.com and www.caitlinselfnutrition.com.

For the steak:
1 pound flank steak
1 teaspoon fish sauce
(gluten free: fish sauce is usually but not always gluten free; double check this)
1 Thai chili, thinly sliced (substitute jalapeño if Thai chili is unavailable)
1 clove garlic, minced
1 tablespoon freshly chopped mint
1 tablespoon freshly chopped Thai basil (substitute sweet basil if Thai basil is unavailable)
1 tablespoon freshly chopped cilantro
Salt
Pepper

For the quick pickled veggies:
1 cup matchstick carrots
4 radishes, thinly sliced
1 small jalapeño, thinly sliced
¼ red onion, thinly sliced
¼ cup rice vinegar
1 tablespoon coconut aminos
(see Know Your Ingredients on page 65)

For serving:
Butter lettuce leaves
½ cucumber, sliced
1 avocado, sliced
1 lime
Fresh mint leaves
Fresh basil leaves
Fresh cilantro leaves

Baked Cavatini

Why You'll Love It:
The easy, cheesy goodness of this baked pasta casserole will bring out the kid in you.

Prep Time: 5 minutes | Cook Time: 45 minutes | Total Time: 50 minutes | Yield: 4 servings

Preheat oven to 350°F. Lightly coat the inside of a 3 quart casserole dish with olive oil (or other cooking oil).

Cook pasta according to package instructions. Drain and return to the pot or place in a large bowl.

While the pasta is cooking, brown ground beef in a medium saucepan. Break it up with a spoon or spatula while browning to crumble it. Drain grease from beef and return to saucepan.

Add marinara sauce to the beef and stir to combine. Bring to a simmer over medium heat.

Pour meat sauce over cooked pasta. Add most of the pepperoni, reserving some slices for the top. Stir until combined. Transfer mixture to prepared casserole dish and spread evenly in the dish.

Sprinkle mozzarella cheese evenly over pasta mixture. Sprinkle parmesan over mozzarella. Place remaining slices of pepperoni on top.

Bake for 25 to 30 minutes, or until it begins to bubble and the cheese has melted and is slightly brown on the edges.

Olive oil

12 ounces uncooked medium pasta shells (gluten free: substitute gluten free pasta shells, spirals, or elbows)

½ pound ground beef

5 cups marinara sauce

6 ounces sliced pepperoni, divided

12 ounces shredded mozzarella cheese

3 ounces grated parmesan cheese

Mozzarella

KNOW YOUR INGREDIENTS

What are the different types of mozzarella, and how do you use them?

Fresh mozzarella is a soft, moist, and fresh cheese that's best served uncooked. Fresh mozzarella is the type of cheese used in caprese salads, layered with fresh tomatoes and drizzled with balsamic vinegar.

Low moisture mozzarella is aged longer to remove additional moisture. This type of mozzarella is best for preparations that require smooth melting, great "stretch," and the ability to brown nicely in the oven. Baked pasta dishes and pizza are good examples of how to use low moisture mozzarella.

Mozzarella can be made from whole milk or reduced fat milk. *Whole milk mozzarella* has more fat, while *part-skim mozzarella* is more lean. Whole milk mozzarella is known for melting smoothly, while part-skim mozzarella browns more easily. As a home cook, you can use whichever fat level suits your preference. Either whole milk or part-skim mozzarella will work equally well in most recipes. Fresh mozzarella and low moisture mozzarella, on the other hand, are not interchangeable.

Greek Meatball Salad

Why You'll Love It:
This dinner salad combines crisp fresh produce, bright and creamy sauce, and crunchy, savory meatballs to make an exciting meal that's as good as a restaurant could make.

Prep Time: 35 minutes | Cook Time: 30 minutes | Total Time: 1 hour 5 minutes | Yield: 4 servings

For the tzatziki sauce:

Peel cucumber and remove seeds. Lay a cheesecloth on a work surface. Grate cucumber onto the cheesecloth.

Pull up edges of cheesecloth and squeeze liquid from cucumber. Place cheesecloth with cucumber in a sieve or strainer over a bowl.

Sprinkle ¼ teaspoon salt over cucumber. Toss to coat. Allow to set for 30 minutes.

Pull up edges of cheesecloth again and squeeze liquid from cucumber. Transfer cucumber to a medium bowl.

Add remaining ingredients and stir to combine. Cover and chill for at least 1 hour.

For the meatballs:

Heat oven to 350°F. Place a rack in a rimmed baking sheet.

Stir together couscous, egg, mint, garlic, salt, and pepper in a large bowl. Add ground beef and lamb and mix well. Shape into 12 meatballs.

Heat olive oil in a large skillet over medium heat. Brown half of the meatballs, turning to brown evenly. Transfer browned meatballs to rack on baking sheet. Repeat with remaining half of meatballs.

Bake meatballs for 12 to 15 minutes, until cooked through (internal temperature registers 160°F when tested with an instant read thermometer).

For the salad:

Divide romaine, cucumber, tomatoes, and onion equally among 4 plates. Top each with meatballs.

Serve with tzatziki sauce for the dressing.

For the tzatziki sauce:
1 cucumber
½ teaspoon kosher salt, divided
2 cups full-fat Greek yogurt
1 ½ tablespoons fresh lemon juice
1 tablespoon olive oil
1 tablespoon chopped fresh dill
1 garlic clove, minced
⅛ teaspoon fresh ground pepper

For the meatballs:
½ cup cooked couscous, at room temperature or chilled (gluten free: substitute cooked quinoa or rice)
1 egg, lightly beaten
1 tablespoon chopped fresh mint
2 cloves garlic, minced
¼ teaspoon salt
⅛ teaspoon ground black pepper
½ pound ground beef round or chuck
½ pound ground lamb
2 tablespoons olive oil

For the salad:
6 cups torn or chopped romaine lettuce
1 cucumber, peeled and cut into bite-sized chunks
1 cup grape tomatoes, cut in half
½ red onion, sliced

New York Strip Roast

Why You'll Love It:
With just two ingredients and virtually hands-off cooking, this roast can serve a crowd or make wonderful leftovers with no effort at all. All you have to do is put it in the oven and leave it alone 'til it's done.

Prep Time: 5 minutes | Cook Time: 1 hour | Total Time: 1 hour 5 minutes | Yield: 6 to 8 servings

Preheat the oven to 425°F and line a roasting pan with foil for easy cleanup. Place a rack in the roasting pan. (If you don't have a rack, crunch up a long piece of aluminum foil into a loose coil and place it in the roasting pan to serve as a rack.)

Sprinkle 1 tablespoon of steak seasoning all over the roast, gently pressing it on the surface to make it stick. If you have an oven-safe meat thermometer, you may insert it into the thickest part of the roast now, before it goes in the oven.

Place the seasoned roast fatty side up on the roasting rack. Roast for 15 minutes at 425°F.

Reduce the temperature to 325°F and continue cooking for about 45 minutes, or until a meat thermometer reads 135 to 140°F. (Check after 30 minutes in case it cooks faster, or if the roast is slightly smaller.)

Remove roast from oven and let rest for 15 minutes. Slice across the grain to serve.

For the steak seasoning:

¼ cup kosher salt

2 teaspoons ground black pepper

1 teaspoon paprika

1 teaspoon garlic powder

½ teaspoon onion powder

¼ teaspoon ground thyme

For the roast:

3 pounds New York strip roast

1 tablespoon steak seasoning

KNOW YOUR INGREDIENTS

Bison meat is becoming more popular in the United States. Ground bison is available in many grocery stores and can be a great alternative to ground beef. Bison meat is higher in protein and iron, and lower in fat, than beef. Bison meat has a very slightly sweet flavor with none of the gamey taste that can be found in some alternative meats.

Try it for meatloaf and burgers, or as an alternative to ground beef in spaghetti dishes, to increase your protein and iron consumption and lower your fat intake without sacrificing the slightest amount of flavor. You might even come to prefer the flavor of bison!

Bison Meatloaf

Why You'll Love It:
Bison has a slightly sweet flavor that makes it perfect for meatloaf that's glazed with a touch of ketchup. Plus, ground bison has more iron and less fat than ground beef.

Prep Time: 5 minutes | Cook Time: 45 minutes | Total Time: 50 minutes | Yield: 4 servings

Preheat the oven to 375°F.

In a large mixing bowl, combine the cracker crumbs, water, salt, black pepper, and 2 tablespoons of ketchup. Mix well with a fork until a chunky paste is formed.

Add the ground bison to the bowl. Mix with the paste until thoroughly combined.

Place the mixture into an 8 by 8 square pan and pat down until even. Use a brush to glaze the top of the loaf with the remaining ketchup.

Bake at 375°F for about 40 minutes, or until the internal temperature in the center of the meatloaf reaches at least 160°F. Remove from oven, let cool for 5 minutes, then serve.

¼ cup cheddar cracker crumbs (gluten free: substitute gluten free cheddar crackers or use gluten free seasoned bread crumbs)

1 tablespoon water

¼ teaspoon salt

⅛ teaspoon finely ground black pepper

¼ cup ketchup, divided

1 pound ground bison

Quick Spaghetti and Meatballs

Why You'll Love It:
The name says it all. Quick cooking meatballs get a nice brown crust in the oven while the pasta cooks; in no time at all, dinner is ready!

Prep Time: 10 minutes | Cook Time: 20 minutes | Total Time: 30 minutes | Yield: 4 servings

Preheat oven to 400°F. Mix together the cracker crumbs, Italian seasoning, garlic powder, salt, and grated parmesan cheese. Set aside.

In a large mixing bowl, combine the ground sirloin and the tomato sauce. Mix until the sauce is evenly distributed through the beef. Then, mix in the cracker crumb mixture until it is evenly distributed through the beef.

Form meatballs approximately 1 ½ to 2 inches in diameter. You should end up with about 12 meatballs. Place the meatballs evenly in a baking dish so that they are not touching. (You can line this baking dish with parchment paper to prevent sticking, if desired.)

Bake for 20 minutes at 400°F, or until the internal temperature of a meatball measured with an instant read thermometer equals 160°F or greater.

While the meatballs are baking, prepare the spaghetti according to the package directions. Drain the spaghetti, then add the spaghetti sauce to the pot to warm it up. Add the spaghetti and stir to coat. When the meatballs are done, add them to the pot and stir gently to coat with sauce, then serve.

For the meatballs:

⅓ cup seasoned bread crumbs (gluten free: substitute gluten free seasoned bread crumbs)

2 teaspoons Italian seasoning

¼ teaspoon garlic powder

¼ teaspoon salt

⅓ cup grated parmesan cheese

1 pound lean ground beef

⅓ cup spaghetti sauce

For the spaghetti:

1 pound spaghetti (gluten free: substitute gluten free spaghetti)

2 cups spaghetti sauce

Chili Cheese Potato Parfait

Why You'll Love It:
Once you know how to make the base chili recipe, you can use it any way you like. This recipe layers chili with mashed potatoes and cheese sauce, but you could also use the chili for chili baked potatoes, chili nachos, or chili mac.

Prep Time: 5 minutes | Cook Time: 10 minutes | Total Time: 15 minutes | Yield: 4 servings

Sauté the ground beef in a large skillet over medium heat until brown and completely cooked, about 10 minutes.

Evenly sprinkle the chili powder and chipotle chile powder over the cooked ground beef. Add the tomato sauce and stir. Bring to a boil, then reduce heat to low and simmer for 5 minutes. Chop the tomato.

Heat the mashed potatoes and cheese sauce. In the parfait glasses (or in bowls or large mugs, if you don't have parfait glasses), build up even layers of mashed potatoes, chili, cheese sauce, and chopped tomatoes. Finish each glass with a scoop of mashed potatoes drizzled with cheese sauce and garnished with chopped tomatoes. Serve immediately.

Special Equipment: 4 large parfait glasses (optional)

1 pound lean ground beef

2 tablespoons chili powder

½ teaspoon chipotle chile powder

8 ounces tomato sauce

2 ½ cups mashed potatoes (substitute mashed cauliflower for a lower carb version)

1 cup cheese sauce (gluten free: double check that the cheese sauce is gluten free)

1 tomato

Smash Burgers

Why You'll Love It:
The smash technique ensures quick cooking and a lovely brown crust on the outside of the burger. By smashing only on one side, you won't lose any moisture. You can substitute ground sirloin or even ground bison for the ground chuck, if you prefer.

Prep Time: 15 minutes | **Cook Time:** 14 minutes (assuming that 2 burgers can cook at a time)
Total Time: 29 minutes | **Yield:** 4 burgers

Preheat a nonstick skillet over medium-high heat. Divide the ground chuck into 3 or 4 equal pieces. Without handling the meat too much, shape each piece into a ball.

When you are ready to cook, but no sooner, season the patties with a little pinch of salt and pepper. Have your turner at hand for the next step.

Place a ball in the skillet. Smash it down flat as firmly and evenly as you can, flattening the meat and holding it down for about 10 seconds. You can add another patty if it will fit without crowding the pan. Cook the patties for 4 minutes, then flip them over. (Don't smash them this time!)

Cook for 3 more minutes, or until the internal temperature reaches 160°F as measured with an instant read thermometer. Remove from the skillet with a clean turner to a hamburger bun. Add a slice of American cheese and other burger toppings as desired.

1 pound ground chuck

Salt

Pepper

4 hamburger buns (gluten free: substitute gluten free hamburger buns)

Toppings:

American cheese

Dill pickle chips

Mustard

Ketchup

Boliche (Cuban Stuffed Roast)

Why You'll Love It:
This roast is literally stuffed with flavor. The work of preparing boliche occurs at the beginning and the end; the middle time period, when it cooks, requires only the occasional task of turning the meat to cook on the other side. Try it on your day off to fill your home with a heavenly scent.

Prep Time: 30 minutes | Cook Time: 2 hours | Total Time: 2 hours 30 minutes
Yield: 6 to 8 servings

Place chorizo, garlic, and olives in a food processor fitted with a knife blade. Process until garlic and olives are finely chopped.

Cut a hole in the center of the roast lengthwise. Do this by inserting a long knife in the center until it is almost through to the end. Then turn the knife while it is in the roast to open up the pocket. Repeat with inserting the knife again at a 90 degree angle. You want to try and make as large of a hole as you can in the center of the roast.

Stuff the chorizo mixture into the hole in the roast. If you have a long and narrow roast, you may need to cut the roast open in order to get the stuffing all the way to the end. You will need to tie the roast back together with kitchen twine.

You may not be able to stuff all the chorizo mixture into the roast. You can form the extra into patties and cook them in a skillet. They make great breakfast sausage patties.

Season the roast with salt and pepper.

Heat the oil in a large Dutch oven over medium-high heat. Place the roast in the Dutch oven and brown on all sides. Transfer browned roast to a plate.

continued on next page...

Special Equipment: Food processor

8 ounces Spanish chorizo, casings removed

6 garlic cloves, peeled and chopped

¼ cup pimento stuffed green olives, chopped

3 pound eye of round roast

Salt and pepper

2 tablespoons olive oil

1 large onion, chopped

½ cup dry red wine

Juice of 1 orange

Juice of 1 lemon

Juice of ½ lime

14.5 ounce can diced tomatoes

½ cup low sodium beef broth, plus more if needed

2 bay leaves

Cornstarch to thicken gravy, if desired

Boliche
(Cuban Stuffed Roast)
continued

Reduce heat to medium. Add onions and cook, stirring occasionally, until softened and becoming translucent, about 5 minutes.

Add wine, orange, lemon, and lime juice. Use a wooden spoon to stir and scrape up the browned bits from the bottom of the Dutch oven.

Add diced tomatoes and stir. Add roast back to the Dutch oven.

Add enough beef broth to make the cooking liquid 1-inch deep. Add bay leaves.

Bring to a boil then cover and reduce heat to simmer.

Cook for 1 hour and 45 minutes, turning roast every 20 minutes.

Use an instant-read thermometer to make sure the stuffing is cooked through (160°F). The roast will be cooked to well done.

Transfer roast to a cutting board and cover loosely with aluminum foil.

Use a blender to puree the cooking liquid. You may need to do this in batches. Do not fill a blender over ⅔ full with hot liquids because they will expand while blending.

Return puree to the Dutch oven and bring to a boil.

If a thicker gravy is desired, stir together 1 tablespoon cornstarch with 1 tablespoon water to make a slurry. Slowly pour a little of the slurry into the gravy while stirring rapidly. Add only as much needed to desired thickness.

Remove kitchen twine if used to tie the roast.

Slice roast into ½-inch thick slices. Serve with gravy.

KNOW YOUR INGREDIENTS

Mexican chorizo is made from pork and is uncooked. It comes in sausage casings and is strongly flavored with spicy chiles. Typically, to prepare Mexican chorizo, you remove it from its casing and cook it in a skillet. It can then be added to tacos, scrambled eggs, and so on. Mexican chorizo can be found shelved with refrigerated Mexican foods like crema and cheese, or with uncooked sausages.

Spanish chorizo, on the other hand, is dried and cured or semi-cured. Because it is ready to eat, it can be served with the casings on as part of a tapas plate, or it can be sliced, chopped, or crumbled before adding to main course recipes as a flavoring ingredient. There are smoked and unsmoked varieties of Spanish chorizo available, as well as versions that are sweet or spicy. You can often find Spanish chorizo alongside other fully cooked sausages in the grocery store.

Although Mexican chorizo and Spanish chorizo are similar in terms of color, they have very different flavors and should not be substituted for one another.

Pork

One Pan Roasted Asian Pork and Vegetables

Why You'll Love It:
This recipe cooks all together in one pan, in just one hour. The flavor of Chinese five spice powder complements the peanut satay-flavored broccoli and Brussels sprouts.

Prep Time: 10 minutes | Cook Time: 1 hour | Total Time: 1 hour 10 minutes
Yield: 4 servings

Preheat the oven to 425°F.

Cut the large stem from each stalk of broccoli. Cut the remaining heads of broccoli into large florets. Trim the ends of the Brussels sprouts by cutting away the brown part of the stem end.

Place the vegetables in a 13-inch by 9-inch baking pan. Drizzle the olive oil over the vegetables, then use your hands to mix until coated.

Rub the five spice powder all over the pork, then place the pork on top of the vegetables in the baking pan. If the pork has a fattier side, turn that side to face up (it will self-baste as the fat melts).

Roast for approximately 1 hour, or until the internal temperature in the thickest part of the pork tenderloin is 160°F. Remove the pan from the oven and let everything rest for 5 minutes.

Remove the pork to a cutting board for slicing. Dot the peanut sauce over the vegetables and mix to coat. Serve sliced pork with vegetables and extra peanut sauce for dipping, if desired.

1 pound fresh Brussels sprouts

1 bunch of fresh broccoli

1 tablespoon olive oil

2 tablespoons five spice powder

2 to 3 pounds pork tenderloin

2 tablespoons peanut satay sauce, plus extra for dipping (gluten free: double check that this ingredient is gluten free)

Pork Chops with Sauerkraut

Why You'll Love It:
This recipe combines the techniques of browning and braising. Browning gives the meat flavor, while braising helps it become tender.

Prep Time: 5 minutes | Cook Time: 35 minutes | Total Time: 40 minutes | Yield: 4 servings

Season the pork chops with a pinch of salt and pepper.

In a large skillet over medium-high heat, add a thin layer of oil. Heat until almost smoking. Add the chops to the pan and brown both sides, about 2 to 3 minutes on each side.

Add the sauerkraut to the skillet. Bring to a boil, cover, and turn down the heat to low.

Simmer for 30 to 40 minutes until the chops are tender. Serve immediately.

4 to 6 thin cut pork chops

Salt

Pepper

Cooking oil

16 ounces sauerkraut, liquid included

Gnocchi

KNOW YOUR INGREDIENTS

Gnocchi are Italian dumplings made from potatoes and flour. Some gnocchi are made gluten free by substituting alternative flours, like corn flour, for the wheat flour. Either way, gnocchi are a delicious alternative to pasta. They cook very rapidly in salted boiling water, which means they're an excellent choice for quick meals. All you need is a sauce. Gnocchi can be enjoyed with pesto sauce, tomato sauce, cheese sauce, or just some butter and herbs; if it could be served over pasta, it would probably work to serve it over gnocchi.

Gnocchi with Italian Sausage

Why You'll Love It:
Comfort food at its best, this rich and savory dish of gnocchi, crumbled Italian sausage, and veggies cooks up quickly and will satisfy you right down to your toes.

Prep Time: 10 minutes | Cook Time: 20 minutes | Total Time: 30 minutes | Yield: 4 servings

Cook the gnocchi according to the package directions. While the gnocchi are cooking, prepare the sauce.

In a large skillet, sauté sausage with olive oil until fully cooked. Add the sliced mushrooms and cook for a minute, then add chicken stock and bring to a boil.

Add tomato, escarole and olives and cook for 1 minute more. Add butter. When the sauce is done, taste it and season with salt and pepper if needed.

Drain the gnocchi and add to the sauce. Stir the gnocchi and sauce together. Divide into equal portions, garnish with grated parmesan cheese, and serve.

1 pound gnocchi (gluten free: substitute gluten free gnocchi)

1 pound Italian sausage, crumbled

2 tablespoons olive oil

1 cup sliced mushrooms

1 ½ cups chicken stock

½ cup kalamata olives, pits removed

2 cups escarole

1 cup chopped tomato

8 tablespoons unsalted butter

Salt

Pepper

Grated parmesan cheese

Pulled Pork in the Oven

Why You'll Love It:
Once you get the pork marinated and into the oven, you just kick back and let it cook. When it's done, you can use the resulting pulled pork for sandwiches (just add barbecue sauce) or tacos.

**Prep Time: 5 minutes | Inactive Time: 8 hours, or overnight | Cook Time: 4 hours
Total Time: 12 hours 5 minutes | Yield: 4 to 6 servings**

Mix the dry rub ingredients together to make a dry rub. Sprinkle 2 tablespoons of dry rub evenly all over the pork brisket, patting it as you go to make the rub stick to the pork. Cover and marinate overnight, or 8 hours, in the refrigerator.

When ready to cook, preheat the oven to 450°F. Choose an oven safe pot that's close to the size of the pork brisket (neither too big nor too small). The pot should have a lid, but you will not need it for the first step of cooking. Gently place the marinated pork brisket in the pot with the fattiest side on top. Leave the pot uncovered.

Roast, uncovered, for 15 minutes at 450°F. While roasting, add the tomato paste to a bowl. Whisk in the water until you have a smooth liquid.

Remove the pot from the oven and carefully pour the liquid into the bottom of the pot. Cover the pot with its lid and return the pot to the oven. Turn the oven temperature down to 300°F.

Cook at 300°F for about 4 hours, or until the pork falls apart easily when gently tugged with a fork. (4 hours is the typical minimum time; if your roast is larger or is not boneless, just keep on cooking it until it becomes fall-apart tender.)

For the dry rub:

¼ cup smoked paprika

2 tablespoons brown sugar

2 tablespoons kosher salt

1 teaspoon black pepper

1 teaspoon ground cumin

For the pork:

2 ½ pounds boneless pork shoulder picnic roast

2 tablespoons dry rub

2 tablespoons tomato paste

1 cup water

Roast Pork Loin Filet with Whole Mushrooms

Why You'll Love It:
This recipe magically makes its own sauce. Once the roast is in the oven, your work is done; just sit back and relax!

Prep Time: 5 minutes | Cook Time: 1 hour | Total Time: 1 hour 5 minutes | Yield: 6 to 8 servings

Preheat the oven to 375°F and line a 13 by 9 inch pan with foil for easy cleanup. Rub all of the spice mix all over the pork loin filet, then place the pork loin filet in the lined pan.

Rinse the mushrooms thoroughly. Remove the stems from the mushrooms and discard. Toss the mushrooms with the olive oil plus a pinch of salt and pepper.

Place the mushrooms in the pan, with the open cup turned upwards, surrounding the pork loin filet.

Put the pan in the oven and bake for about one hour, or until the internal temperature of the pork reaches 160°F. The mushrooms will look very dark, but they will not burn.

Let the pork rest for 5 minutes, then slice and serve with mushrooms.

For the spice mix:

1 teaspoon ground cumin

1 teaspoon ground ginger

¾ teaspoon ground black pepper

½ teaspoon ground cinnamon

½ teaspoon cayenne

½ teaspoon ground allspice

¼ teaspoon ground cloves

¼ teaspoon salt

For the pork and mushrooms:

3 pounds pork loin filet

1 tablespoon extra virgin olive oil

1 pound baby bella mushrooms

Salt

Black pepper

Irish Bacon and Cheese Frittata

Why You'll Love It:
Frittatas are quick to make and quite flexible regarding ingredients. You can use just about any cheese or cooked meat you like. Add a handful of veggies—like cooked mushrooms, broccoli, or bell peppers—to increase nutrition and round out the meal.

Prep Time: 10 minutes | Cook Time: 20 minutes | Total Time: 30 minutes | Yield: 4 servings

Preheat the oven to 375°F. In a medium bowl, whisk together the eggs and cream. Season the mixture with a pinch of salt and pepper, add 3/4 cup shredded cheese, and stir to combine.

Heat the skillet over medium-high heat. Distribute chopped Irish bacon evenly around the skillet, then pour the egg mixture over everything. Sprinkle the remaining ¾ cup shredded cheese over the top. Cook on the stovetop for 2 minutes, and then transfer skillet to the oven. Bake for 20 minutes or until the eggs have set.

Cool in the pan for 10 minutes. Slice and enjoy. Leftovers can be refrigerated and served cold or reheated.

Special Equipment: Large oven safe skillet

8 eggs

¼ cup heavy cream, half-and-half, or milk

Salt

Pepper

1 ½ cups shredded Kerrygold Skellig, Kildery, Dubliner, or cheddar cheese, divided (substitute sharp white cheddar if you can't find any of these)

1 ½ cups cooked chopped Irish bacon or Canadian bacon

Bacon

KNOW YOUR INGREDIENTS

You're probably familiar with *American bacon*, a type of bacon that comes from the pork belly and is streaked with plenty of fat. But did you know that there are several other kinds of bacon?

Irish bacon or *English bacon* is traditionally cut from the loin. It has a texture similar to ham, and sometimes comes with a strip of fat around the outside of each slice.

Canadian bacon also comes from the loin, often in round slices. Its texture is similar to ham and it has a slightly sweet flavor. Canadian bacon is usually lightly brined and, on occasion, can be smoked.

Irish, English, and Canadian bacon may be substituted for one another. Use caution when attempting to substitute American bacon for Irish, English, or Canadian bacon. American bacon has much more fat—not to mention fat that liquefies upon cooking—and it's quite salty.

Corn and Andouille Sausage Chowder

Why You'll Love It:
One pot and one hour are all you need for thick, creamy, hearty chowder filled with corn, potatoes, and andouille sausage.

Prep Time: 10 minutes | Cook Time: 45 minutes | Total Time: 54 minutes | Yield: 4 to 6 servings

In a large pot, brown the sausage over medium heat for about 3 minutes. Add the butter and chopped potatoes, then stir until the butter is completely melted and the potatoes are coated. Sprinkle the flour over the mixture then stir again, cooking for about 1 minute. It may look lumpy, but that's OK; it will smooth out completely during the cooking process.

Pour in the stock and bring to a boil. Boil for 10 to 15 minutes, stirring occasionally to prevent sticking, until the potatoes are fully cooked and break up easily. Use a large fork to break up some of the larger potato pieces into smaller pieces.

Add all the corn and creamed corn. Add the half-and-half. Add a pinch of thyme, ground black pepper, and paprika. Simmer for about 7 minutes, stirring occasionally to prevent sticking.

Taste the chowder. Depending on the amount of salt in the sausage, broth, and corn, you may or may not need to add more salt to taste. Start with a small amount if needed, letting it dissolve completely with vigorous stirring, then add more a little at a time, stirring after each addition, until it tastes properly salted to you.

In a small bowl, whisk the cornstarch with 1 tablespoon of water until the mixture is completely smooth. Stir the smooth mixture of cornstarch and water into the chowder, then let the chowder simmer for 10 minutes. Remove from heat, let it cool slightly, then serve.

12 ounces andouille sausage, sliced into rounds (equal to about 2 ½ cups)

2 tablespoons butter

2 medium potatoes, peeled and chopped

¼ cup all purpose flour (gluten free: substitute gluten free baking mix flour)

4 cups chicken stock

2 cups corn

1 cup creamed corn

1 cup half-and-half

Pinch of dried thyme

Pinch of ground black pepper

Pinch of paprika

Salt

1 tablespoon cornstarch

Sherry Apple Pork Roast

Why You'll Love It:
This juicy pork roast tantalizes with its sweet, tangy, and savory flavors. Try making it on a cool fall day to appreciate its rich autumnal aroma.

Prep Time: 10 minutes | Cook Time: 1 hour 50 minutes | Total Time: 2 hours | Yield: 4 to 6 servings

---

Preheat oven to 350°F.

Sprinkle pork with a pinch of salt and pepper.

Heat oil in a medium-size Dutch oven (about 5-quart) over medium-high heat until almost smoking.

Add pork to the pan and sear to brown on all sides, about 2 to 3 minutes per side.

Remove pork from the pan and place on a plate.

Reduce heat to medium and add onion. Cook until onions have softened, about 5 minutes.

Add garlic. Stir and cook for 1 minute.

Stir together sherry, orange juice, and brown sugar.

Return pork to the pan along with apple slices and sherry mixture. Cover and place in the oven.

Roast for 1 ½ hours, or until pork has an internal temperature of at least 160°F.

Place pork on a cutting board and let set for 15 minutes.

Put apples, onions, and all pan juices in a blender. Blend until liquefied and pour sauce back into pan. Bring sauce to a simmer then reduce heat to low to keep warm until serving.

Slice pork and place on a serving platter. Serve with sauce.

---

2 ½ pound boneless pork loin roast

Salt

Pepper

2 tablespoons vegetable or canola oil

1 medium onion, sliced

2 cooking apples, Granny Smith recommended, cored and sliced

1 garlic clove, minced

¾ cup dry sherry

½ cup orange juice

2 tablespoons light brown sugar

Poultry

Mushroom and Swiss Stuffed Turkey Burgers

Why You'll Love It:
Ground turkey isn't just for health nuts. When stuffed with sautéed mushrooms and Swiss cheese, turkey burgers become just as good as hamburgers.

Prep Time: 15 minutes | Cook Time: 20 minutes | Total Time: 35 minutes | Yield: 4 servings

For the mushrooms:

Olive oil

8 ounces baby bella mushrooms, sliced

½ cup beef broth, plus extra 1 tablespoon

1 teaspoon cornstarch

For the burgers:

Olive oil

1 pound lean ground turkey

4 slices Swiss cheese

For the mushrooms:

Drizzle olive oil into a large skillet and heat over medium heat. Add the sliced mushrooms and cook until tender, about 8 minutes.

Add ½ cup of beef broth to the pan. In a small bowl, whisk the cornstarch with a tablespoon of beef broth until a very smooth liquid is formed (no lumps).

Add the cornstarch liquid to the pan, then stir and cook on low for about 2 minutes until the gravy thickens and becomes glossy.

Split the finished mushrooms and gravy in half, into two separate bowls: one for filling the inside of the burgers, and one to be set aside for topping the finished burgers.

For the burgers:

Fold each slice of Swiss in half, then fold in half again, making each slice into a thick square-shaped stack of Swiss. 4 slices of cheese = 4 stacks.

Divide the pound of turkey into 8 equal parts. For each burger, flatten 2 parts into separate patties. Top one patty with a spoonful of mushrooms with gravy and place a Swiss cheese stack on top. Gently cover the first patty with the second patty and pinch the edges to seal, tamping gently to even out the thickness. Repeat until you have 4 stuffed turkey burgers ready to cook.

Drizzle olive oil into a skillet and heat it to medium heat. Cook the burgers in the skillet for about 5 minutes on each side or until the meat reaches 165°F. If the pan begins to get too hot, reduce the heat slightly so the meat doesn't burn or stick.

Serve on buns and top with the mushrooms and gravy that you set aside earlier.

Yogurt Marinated Chicken

Why You'll Love It:
A two ingredient marinade transforms chicken overnight, then it cooks up in just 15 minutes. It's one of the fastest and most flavorful main courses you'll ever make.

Prep Time: 5 minutes | **Inactive Time:** 8 hours, or overnight | **Cook Time:** 15 minutes
Total Time: 8 hours 20 minutes | **Yield:** 4 to 6 servings

Stir 3 tablespoons garam masala into the yogurt until smooth and well combined. Coat the chicken all over with the spiced yogurt (it is easy to spread it on the chicken with the back of a spoon) and place it in a covered pan in the refrigerator. Discard any remaining spiced yogurt. Marinate for 8 hours, or overnight.

Scrape all the yogurt off the chicken and discard the yogurt. Brush olive oil all over each piece of chicken. Preheat a skillet or grill pan over medium heat. Cook each piece of chicken on one side for 5 to 6 minutes, then turn and cook on the other side for another 5 to 6 minutes.

For the garam masala:

1 ½ tablespoons ground cumin

1 ½ tablespoon ground coriander

1 teaspoon ground cinnamon

½ teaspoon ground cloves

½ teaspoon ground nutmeg

¼ teaspoon ground black pepper

¼ teaspoon ground cardamom

For the chicken:

3 tablespoons garam masala

1 cup plain whole Greek yogurt

1 ½ pounds chicken breasts, butterflied or thin sliced

¼ cup olive oil

Buffalo Chicken Quesadillas

Why You'll Love It:
The easy, cheesy goodness of this baked pasta casserole will bring out the kid in you. These quesadillas serve up spicy goodness in record time. Bold Buffalo flavor and traditional accompaniments make a home-cooked meal feel like a night out.

Prep Time: 5 minutes | Cook Time: 10 minutes | Total Time: 15 minutes | Yield: 4 small quesadillas

Preheat a large nonstick pan on medium low heat for a few minutes.

Toss the chicken with the buffalo wing sauce to coat. Separately, toss the shredded cheese with the blue cheese crumbles.

When the pan is hot, place 4 corn tortillas in the pan (do not overlap).

Sprinkle cheese and chicken on each tortilla in the pan, then add another tortilla and press down. Cook the quesadilla until there are brown spots on the outside of the corn tortilla on the bottom, about 3 to 5 minutes, then use a large turner to flip the quesadilla over. Continue cooking until the cheese is melted and the corn tortilla on the bottom has brown spots.

Repeat steps 2 through 4 to make the rest of the quesadillas.

Serve immediately with carrot sticks or celery sticks on the side, and blue cheese dressing for dipping.

2 cups cooked diced or pulled chicken

¼ cup Buffalo wing sauce

1 ½ cups shredded quesadilla melting cheese

2 tablespoons blue cheese crumbles

8 corn tortillas

Carrot sticks or celery sticks

Blue cheese dressing

Apple Cranberry Pecan Chicken Salad

Why You'll Love It:
Ready in just five minutes, this delightful chicken salad combines creamy, crunchy, sweet, and savory in every bite. It can be served on salad, on sandwiches, or enjoyed all on its own.

Prep Time: 5 minutes | Cook Time: 0 minutes | Total Time: 5 minutes | Yield: 4 servings

Remove the apple core and chop the apple into small pieces. Chop the chicken into small pieces. Add the chopped apple, chopped chicken, pecans, and dried cranberries to a mixing bowl.

Add the mayonnaise and mix well, until everything is evenly coated. Add a little more mayonnaise (1 tablespoon at a time) if the mixture is too dry. Taste, and add salt a pinch at a time (if needed), stirring well.

¾ pound cooked chicken

1 apple, such as Honeycrisp

¼ cup mayonnaise

½ cup chopped pecans

⅓ cup dried cranberries

Salt

Spinach Cream Cheese Stuffed Chicken Breasts Wrapped in Bacon

Why You'll Love It:
These magnificent stuffed chicken breasts are beautiful and delicious. You'll feel like you're treating yourself to a special meal when you dig in to the layers of chicken, cheese stuffing, and crispy bacon.

Prep Time: 15 minutes | **Cook Time:** 45 minutes | **Total Time:** 1 hour | **Yield:** 4 servings

Preheat oven to 375°F.

Place each chicken breast on a flat surface. With your hand placed flat on each piece, cut about ¾ quarter of the way through (be careful not to cut all the way through).

Blend spinach, cream cheese, parmesan cheese, chives and garlic in a medium bowl.

Spoon ¼ of cheese mixture into the middle of the cut chicken breasts.

Wrap each stuffed breast with 2 slices of bacon.

Arrange chicken breasts on baking sheet.

Cook for 30 to 40 minutes, then turn the temperature up to 400°F (or on low broil) and cook for about 15 more minutes to get the bacon nice and crispy.

- 4 chicken breasts
- 10 ounce package frozen chopped spinach, thawed and squeezed dry
- 4 ounces reduced fat cream cheese, room temperature
- ¼ cup parmesan cheese
- 2 tablespoons chopped fresh chives, sliced thin
- 4 cloves garlic
- 8 slices bacon

Recipe contributed by Sherri Hagymas, author of To Simply Inspire.

Turkey Reuben Panini

Why You'll Love It:
Fast and fun, this turkey variation on the classic Reuben sandwich is a smart way to use up leftover turkey.

Prep Time: 5 minutes | Cook Time: 5 minutes | Total Time: 10 minutes | Yield: variable

Heat the panini maker.

Spread plenty of dressing on one side of two slices of rye bread. On one slice add a slice of Swiss cheese, then a layer of turkey. Squeeze the liquid from the sauerkraut and place ¼ cup of sauerkraut on top of turkey. Place another slice of Swiss cheese on top. Cover with the other slice of bread with the dressing on the inside. Spray the outside of the bread with the olive oil spray.

Place the sandwich in the panini maker and lower the top down. Grill for about 5 minutes, until toasted. If you don't have a panini maker, simply grill the sandwiches in a skillet over medium heat until they are golden brown on both sides and the cheese melts.

Special Equipment: Panini maker

8 slices rye bread (gluten free: substitute gluten free rye-style bread or your favorite gluten free bread)

½ cup Thousand Island dressing, divided

1 pound roasted turkey, sliced thin, divided

1 cup sauerkraut, divided

8 slices Swiss cheese

Olive oil spray

Grilled Chicken Caesar Salad

Why You'll Love It:
Grilled chicken takes the classic Caesar salad to a whole new level and makes it a complete meal worthy of any dinner table.

Prep Time: 15 minutes | Cook Time: 10 minutes | Total Time: 25 minutes | Yield: 4 servings

Special Equipment: Grill pan

For the dressing:

1 garlic clove chopped

1 or 2 anchovy fillets chopped

3 tablespoons fresh lemon juice

1 tablespoon white wine vinegar

1 ½ teaspoon Dijon mustard

½ teaspoon Worcestershire sauce

⅓ cup mayonnaise

½ cup olive oil

For the salad:

1 pound boneless chicken tenders or breasts

Olive oil

Salt

Pepper

1 to 2 bags or 1 to 3 heads Romaine lettuce, washed

Parmesan cheese

Croutons (gluten free: substitute gluten free croutons or parmesan crisps)

For the dressing:

Add all dressing ingredients except olive oil to a blender. Turn on the blender and slowly pour in the olive oil as it is blending. Blend until combined and the oil is fully incorporated.

For the salad:

Heat a grill pan over medium-high heat. As the pan is warming, place the chicken between 2 sheets of plastic wrap and pound until about ½-inch thick or a little less. (The thinner the chicken, the faster it will cook). Remove the chicken from the plastic, coat with olive oil and season with a pinch of salt and pepper.

Add the chicken to the heated pan and grill about 4 to 5 minutes on each side or until chicken is browned and cooked through. Transfer the chicken to a cutting board. Allow chicken to rest for about 5 minutes then cut into bite-sized pieces.

If the romaine lettuce is not pre-chopped, chop it and place it in a large bowl. If pre-chopped, add it to a large bowl. Sprinkle some parmesan cheese over the lettuce. Add some dressing and toss to coat the lettuce with the dressing. It is best to add a little at a time to avoid adding too much.

Transfer the lettuce to plates. Top the lettuce with chicken pieces, croutons and some additional parmesan cheese. Serve immediately.

Tortilla Chip Crusted Turkey Cutlets

Why You'll Love It:
Turkey doesn't have to be boring. With a tortilla chip crust, turkey cutlets become crispy, crunchy party food.

Prep Time: 10 minutes | Cook Time: 15 minutes | Total Time: 25 minutes | Yield: 4 servings

Preheat oven to 400°F. Place a wire rack in a rimmed baking sheet.

Whisk together eggs, water, cumin, and garlic.

Dip cutlets in egg mixture then dredge in crushed chips.

Place coated cutlets on wire rack.

Bake for 15 minutes, or until cooked through (no longer pink in center and 165°F internal temperature).

Serve with salsa or picante sauce.

2 large eggs

1 tablespoon water

¼ teaspoon ground cumin

1 garlic clove, crushed

1 pound turkey cutlets, about 1/4 inch thick

2 cups crushed tortilla chips (gluten free: make sure the chips are gluten free)

Salsa or picante sauce, to serve

Seafood

Cedar Plank Salmon

Why You'll Love It:
Cedar plank salmon looks fancy, but it's really quite simple. Don't tell your dinner guests how easy it was; let them think you are a master chef.

Inactive Time: 1 hour to soak the planks | **Prep Time:** 15 minutes | **Cook Time:** 25 minutes
Total Time: 1 hour 40 minutes | **Yield:** 4 servings

Soak the cedar planks in water for 1 hour. When they're almost done soaking, begin preheating the oven to 350°F.

While the oven is preheating, make a brine for the salmon by combining 2 cups of water with 2 tablespoons of salt. Soak the salmon in the brine for 10 minutes while the oven preheats.

Remove the cedar planks from the water and shake off excess water. Remove the salmon from the brine and gently pat to remove excess brine. Sprinkle the salmon rub all over the salmon (you'll use all of it).

Place a flat rack on a baking sheet (you can line the baking sheet with foil first, for easy cleanup, if desired). Place the soaked planks on the rack. Put the baking sheet with the rack and planks on it in the oven for 5 minutes to heat up.

Remove the baking sheet with the rack and planks on it. Place the rubbed salmon on the hot planks, skin side down if skin is present; if the end of a salmon filet is thinner than the center, you can gently fold the thin end under so that the salmon cooks more evenly. Return the baking sheet to the oven. Bake for 20 to 25 minutes, or until desired doneness is reached. (Salmon is fully cooked when it flakes easily with a fork.)

Optional: glaze salmon fillets with melted butter and sprinkle on chopped fresh dill just before serving.

Special Equipment: 2 cedar grilling planks

For the salmon:

2 tablespoons salt, for the brine

1 pound salmon fillets

For the rub:

1 tablespoon brown sugar

½ teaspoon kosher salt

2 teaspoons ancho chili powder

1 teaspoon ground cumin

½ teaspoon ground black pepper

For the garnish:

1 tablespoon melted butter, optional

1 tablespoon chopped dill, optional

Amalfi Coast Risotto

Why You'll Love It:
This risotto is a taste of one of the most beautiful regions of Italy. Its delicate flavors of white wine and fresh lemon will transport you with every bite.

Prep Time: 5 minutes | **Cook Time:** 35 minutes | **Total Time:** 40 minutes | **Yield:** 4 servings

Thoroughly wash the lemon, then grate half of its zest. Save the zest for later. Juice the whole lemon and set the juice aside.

Melt half the butter in a large pan on low heat; peel and dice the onion, add it to the melted butter and cook until the onion becomes clear, stirring continuously. Add the rice and toast for two minutes, increasing the heat to medium, stirring occasionally.

Add the white wine to the rice, and once it has evaporated add the lemon juice followed by the vegetable stock, one cup at a time, stirring continuously until the rice is fully cooked, about 20 minutes.

Turn the heat off and add the cooked shrimp, lemon zest, and the rest of the butter. Season to taste, if needed, with salt and pepper.

1 unwaxed lemon

2 tablespoons plus 2 teaspoons butter, divided

1 small onion

1 ½ cups arborio rice

½ cup dry white wine

4 cups vegetable stock
(gluten free: double check that the stock is gluten free)

1 pound peeled, cooked shrimp

Salt

Pepper

Recipe contributed by Luisa Ruocco, a London based Italian-British social media food and travel influencer who spends her summers on the Amalfi Coast.

Citrus Chimichurri Shrimp Rice

Why You'll Love It:
*Zesty and herbal chimichurri rice provides a fragrant platform for shrimp.
This dinner tastes like the fresh bounty of springtime.*

Prep Time: 20 minutes | Cook Time: 30 minutes | Total Time: 50 minutes | Yield: 4 servings

For the citrus chimichurri:

Grate 1 tablespoon zest from the orange and place zest in the bowl of a food processor fitted with a knife blade.

Cut away the peel and white pith from the orange. Working over a small bowl, cut orange into segments. Set segments aside to use as a topping for the rice.

Squeeze juice from the orange membrane into the food processor bowl. It should be about 3 tablespoons of orange juice.

Add remaining chimichurri ingredients except olive oil.

Pulse a few times to chop the herbs. Scrape down the sides of the bowl.

Pulse while drizzling in olive oil. Do not over-process or it will become a paste.

Stir in additional olive oil if chimichurri is too thick. It should be a loose sauce.

For the shrimp rice:

Heat oven to 375°F.

Cook rice according to package instructions.

Place shrimp on a rimmed baking sheet. Drizzle olive on shrimp and sprinkle with cumin, salt, and pepper. Toss to coat shrimp with oil and seasonings. Spread out shrimp evenly on baking sheet.

Bake for 6 to 8 minutes, until shrimp are just done.

Spread cooked rice evenly on a serving platter.

Dollop citrus chimichurri over rice. Swirl chimichurri into rice.

Cut orange segments in half.

Cut avocado into bite-sized pieces.

Top rice with shrimp, orange segments, and avocado. Drizzle any juice from the orange over rice (if any in bowl with segments). Serve immediately.

Special Equipment: Food processor

For the citrus chimichurri:

1 navel orange

1 teaspoon grated lemon zest

2 teaspoons fresh lemon juice

3 cups fresh cilantro leaves

2 cups fresh parsley leaves

1 tablespoon fresh thyme leaves

1 tablespoon fresh rosemary leaves

½ teaspoon salt

¼ teaspoon fresh ground pepper

¼ teaspoon red pepper flakes

¼ cup olive oil, plus more if needed

For the shrimp rice:

1 cup long grain white rice

1 pound large shrimp, peeled and deveined

1 teaspoon olive oil

½ teaspoon ground cumin

½ teaspoon salt

¼ teaspoon fresh ground pepper

1 avocado

KNOW YOUR INGREDIENTS

Rice comes in many varieties. Although rice is often referred to by its proportions—long grain, medium grain, or short grain—you can't necessarily tell how the rice should be used based on its inclusion in one of those categories. It's more helpful to know each kind of rice by name.

Long grain white rice is the most commonly seen type of rice in the United States. It has long grains that don't stick together when cooked. Long grain rice is suitable as a side dish or incorporated into a casserole. When a recipe calls for rice without specifying further, long grain white rice is usually what's intended.

Brown rice can be any type of rice (long grain, jasmine, etc.) where the husk is removed but the bran is not. Leaving the bran intact means that the rice will have more nutrients and more fiber than white rice. Brown rice is also chewier and has a nuttier flavor than white rice.

Black rice is similar to brown rice, except that the bran is naturally black or dark brown due to the presence of anthocyanins, which provide deep color and antioxidants.

Sprouted rice retains its bran, like brown rice, but is allowed to germinate before being further processed. The germination process changes the nutritional profile of the rice, and some believe that this process makes sprouted rice even better for you than regular brown rice.

Arborio rice is a medium grain rice that retains a tender yet chewy texture even through a long period of cooking. It's the rice most often used in risotto. With the right cooking technique, arborio rice becomes creamy and thick.

Jasmine rice is a long grain rice with a slightly floral aroma. It's commonly used in Thai cuisine and is a little bit sticky, which allows it to be easily formed into perfect mounds with the use of a small bowl or mold.

Basmati rice is a long grain rice frequently used in Indian cuisine. Basmati rice has a nutty flavor and the individual grains of rice remain separate when cooked, without sticking together.

Sushi rice is a short grain rice that is somewhat sticky when cooked. The best sushi rice comes from Japan, but there are American varieties of sushi rice such as Calrose that work well for most purposes.

Wild rice is the grain of an aquatic grass, like rice, but wild rice is not actually rice. It's a completely different plant species. Wild rice grains are long, shiny, very nutty in flavor, and take longer to cook than rice. Because wild rice never has the bran removed, it retains more nutrients and fiber.

Shrimp

KNOW YOUR INGREDIENTS

Shrimp come from all over the world, in a variety of sizes of colors. How do you know which shrimp to buy?

Most shrimp are flash frozen to keep them fresh while being transported and stored. The "fresh" shrimp in your grocery store seafood case may be fresh, or they may simply have been defrosted ahead of time to look attractive in the seafood case. It's worth asking before you purchase.

The flavor of shrimp depends less on the size and color of the shrimp and more on the diet of the shrimp. Since it's unlikely that you can discover what the shrimp ate, you can focus on finding shrimp that come from better managed waters. For example, shrimp that is wild caught in U.S. waters is usually higher in quality and more sustainable than foreign wild caught or farmed shrimp.

When choosing a size of shrimp to purchase, pay closer attention to the shrimp per pound count. It's more reliable than adjectives like "jumbo" or "colossal," which are not regulated. Very large shrimp are often more expensive per pound. You may be able to purchase shrimp more economically by selecting a slightly smaller size.

Don't miss out on seasonal and regional shrimp varieties. These wild caught specialities are often available only for a limited season and can be one of the best types of local seafood.

Thai Shrimp Curry

Why You'll Love It:
Treat yourself to Thai take-out... at home! This vividly spiced curry is chock-full of shrimp and fresh vegetables that are both tasty and nutritious.

Prep Time: 10 minutes | Cook Time: 15 minutes | Total Time: 25 minutes | Yield: 4 servings

Whisk together coconut milk, chicken stock, curry paste, brown sugar, fish sauce, ginger paste, and lemongrass paste in a bowl.

Heat a large wok or skillet over high heat. Add 1 tablespoon oil and swirl to coat the pan. Add shrimp and stir fry until opaque, about 3 to 4 minutes. Remove shrimp from pan.

Add remaining 1 tablespoon oil to the pan. Add vegetables and stir-fry until crisp-tender, about 4 minutes.

Pour curry sauce over the vegetables. Bring to a boil and cook for 4 minutes.

Stir in shrimp and basil. Cook for an additional minute or until shrimp is cooked through.

Divide rice into 4 bowls and top with Thai shrimp curry. Serve with lime wedges.

1 ½ cups coconut milk

¼ cup chicken stock

3 tablespoons Thai red curry paste

1 tablespoon brown sugar

2 teaspoons fish sauce (gluten free: fish sauce is usually but not always gluten free; double check this)

2 teaspoons ginger paste

2 teaspoons lemongrass paste

2 tablespoons vegetable or canola oil, divided

1 pound large shrimp, peeled and deveined

4 cups assorted cut-up vegetables, such as onion, bell pepper, snow peas, broccoli, carrots, green beans, etc.

2 tablespoons thinly sliced fresh basil, Thai basil recommended

4 cups cooked rice

1 lime, sliced into wedges

Tuna Cakes

Why You'll Love It:
These crispy, crunchy tuna cakes have just four ingredients and they whip up quickly. Kids love them, and grown-ups do, too.

Prep Time: 5 minutes | Cook Time: 20 minutes | Total Time: 25 minutes | Yield: 4 servings

Drain the tuna. Place ½ cup of bread crumbs in a shallow bowl and set aside. Line a large platter or baking sheet with some paper towels and set aside.

In a large skillet, pour in enough canola oil to cover the bottom to a depth of ¼ inch. Preheat the skillet on medium heat while you get the tuna cakes ready to cook.

In a mixing bowl, combine the tuna and the eggs. Stir vigorously until tuna is well coated with eggs. Break up any very large chunks of tuna. Add the remaining 1 cup of bread crumbs and stir vigorously again until the mixture is well combined.

20 ounces solid white albacore tuna, equal to (4) 5 ounce cans

1 ½ cups Italian seasoned bread crumbs, divided (gluten free: substitute gluten free seasoned bread crumbs)

4 large eggs

Canola oil, for frying

Test the heat of the oil by putting a small piece of the mixture into the skillet. If it sizzles and begins cooking immediately, the oil is hot enough.

Scoop up a scant ¼ cup of the mixture into your hand. Gently shape it into a patty. Place the patty in the bowl of bread crumbs, then turn it over to coat the other side in bread crumbs. Carefully slip the patty into the hot oil. Continue to make patties and place them in the skillet until you run out of space.

Cook the patties for about 5 minutes. When the sides facing down are deep golden brown, turn the patties over and continue cooking for another 5 minutes until that side is deep golden brown as well. Remove them from the skillet and place them on the paper towel-covered platter to absorb excess oil.

Continue to make tuna cake patties from the mixture until you've used it up. Serve tuna cakes immediately.

Canned Tuna

KNOW YOUR INGREDIENTS

Canned tuna is very useful as a quick source of protein for meals. There are several types of canned tuna available, so how do you know which type to use for which recipe?

Chunk light tuna is usually the least expensive type of tuna. It has a stronger flavor and a loose texture. Chunk light tuna works well in tuna casseroles and other recipes where a soft, blendable texture is desirable.

Solid white albacore tuna consists of whole tuna steaks fitted into a can. This type of tuna has a milder flavor than chunk light tuna. Its firm flesh is suitable for serving whole over salads, or in any recipe where you would like to have large pieces of tuna rather than having it blend in.

Chunk white albacore is simply solid white albacore that has been pre-cut into smaller chunks before canning.

For the very best in canned tuna, look for sustainably sourced solid white albacore tuna packed in extra virgin olive oil. It may even come in a jar rather than in a can. The small price difference is worth it.

Basil Buttered Shrimp with Vegetables

Why You'll Love It:
Elegantly balanced with contrasting flavors, textures, and garnishes, these shrimp and vegetables are so delectable that they don't even need an accompanying carbohydrate like rice or pasta.

Prep Time: 5 minutes | Cook Time: 20 minutes | Total Time: 25 minutes | Yield: 4 servings

Mash the basil and red pepper flakes into the butter and set aside. Begin heating a grill pan over medium heat. Brush the zucchini and mushrooms with olive oil.

When the grill pan is hot, lay the zucchini slices in the pan. Cook for 5 to 7 minutes on one side, then flip each piece over and cook the other side for about 5 minutes, until fork-tender but not floppy. Repeat with the mushrooms. When done, plate the zucchini and mushrooms for serving and put the flavored butter into the hot grill pan.

Add the shrimp to the hot pan and stir to coat in the melted flavored butter. Cook for about 3 or 4 minutes, until the shrimp are firm and opaque.

When the shrimp are done, divide them equally, topping the previously plated zucchini and mushrooms. Garnish each plate with cherry tomato halves and parmesan cheese, then serve immediately.

½ ounce fresh basil, finely chopped

Pinch of red pepper flakes

2 tablespoons butter, slightly softened

Extra virgin olive oil

2 zucchini, sliced into rounds

8 ounces white mushrooms, halved lengthwise

Parmesan cheese

1 pound shrimp, cleaned and peeled

8 ounces cherry tomatoes, halved lengthwise

Spicy Shrimp Tacos

Why You'll Love It:
Fast food doesn't get any faster than these shrimp tacos topped with a spicy sour cream, cilantro, salsa verde, and crumbled Mexican cheese. Make them when you're in a hurry to be happy.

Prep Time: 5 minutes | Cook Time: 5 minutes | Total Time: 10 minutes | Yield: 8 tacos

Stir together the sour cream and hot sauce to make the spicy sour cream. Put your tortillas or taco shells and choice of toppings in easy reach, ready to use.

Preheat a large nonstick frying pan over medium heat until a drop of water sizzles away when dropped in the pan.

Put the raw shrimp in a bowl with the olive oil. Sprinkle on the chili powder. Toss to coat the shrimp evenly.

Put the shrimp in a single layer in the hot pan. Cook until firm and no longer translucent, stirring as needed, about 3 or 4 minutes.

Equally distribute the shrimp between the tacos and top with your preferred toppings. Drizzle spicy sour cream on each taco. Serve immediately.

For the spicy sour cream:

½ cup sour cream

2 tablespoons hot sauce

For the tacos:

1 pound shrimp, peeled and deveined, tails removed

1 tablespoon chili powder

2 tablespoons olive oil

8 tortillas or taco shells (gluten free: use gluten free tortillas or taco shells)

Toppings:

Chopped fresh cilantro

Salsa verde

½ cup cooked corn kernels (canned corn works fine)

Cotija cheese, also known as Mexican crumbling cheese, or shredded cheese of your choice

Smoked Salmon

KNOW YOUR INGREDIENTS

To make smoked salmon, raw salmon is first brined in salt, then smoked. Cold smoking is accomplished at a low temperature and retains the silky texture of the salmon while adding smokiness. Hot smoking cooks the salmon, giving it a firm and flaky texture.

Lox, on the other hand, is salmon that is cured, but not smoked. Some delis and restaurants serve "lox" that's actually cold smoked salmon. You can tell the difference by the flavor. True lox is salty but not smoky.

When shopping for any type of cured or smoked salmon, avoid brands that use food dye to create a more colorful appearance.

Latkes with Smoked Salmon

> **Why You'll Love It:**
> *These fluffy, crispy potato latkes are piled high with all the best toppings. They're easy to make with shredded potatoes from your grocery store's refrigerator case. You can even use frozen shredded potatoes if they're fully defrosted and pressed with towels to remove excess moisture.*
>
> Prep Time: 5 minutes | Cook Time: 25 minutes | Total Time: 30 minutes
> Yield: 3 to 4 servings, equivalent to 8 or 9 large latkes total

Line a baking sheet with paper towels and place a rack on top of the paper towels.

In a large skillet, add oil to a depth of about ¼ inch. Begin heating the skillet over medium heat while you prepare the latke mix.

In a large mixing bowl, mix the shredded potatoes, eggs, flour, baking powder, and salt thoroughly.

Test the temperature of the oil by placing a small amount of latke mix in the oil. If it sizzles immediately, the oil is hot enough.

Make a latke patty a little smaller than the palm of your hand and carefully place it in the hot oil. Gently press down on the latke with a turner or the back of a large spoon to flatten it out a little more. Continue adding latkes to the skillet until it is just full; don't overcrowd (a large skillet can usually hold 4 large latkes at a time).

Cook the latkes on one side until golden brown, about 6 minutes, then flip and cook on the other side for about 6 minutes until golden brown. Remove the cooked latkes to the rack.

Serve latkes with chilled smoked salmon, sour cream, and chopped fresh dill or chives for topping.

20 ounces shredded potatoes (about 5 cups)

2 eggs

⅓ cup all purpose flour (gluten free: substitute any gluten free flour)

1 teaspoon baking powder

½ teaspoon salt

Canola oil (or your preferred vegetable oil), for frying

4 ounces cold-smoked salmon, also known as Nova salmon

Sour cream

Chopped fresh dill or chives

Tuna Salad Wraps

Why You'll Love It:
If you're in the mood for something lighter, these wraps fill the bill. You'll be amazed by how much a tuna salad improves when you use very high quality tuna packed in olive oil.

Prep Time: 5 minutes | Cook Time: 0 minutes | Total Time: 5 minutes | Yield: 2 wraps

Combine tuna, celery, parsley, lemon zest, pepper, and mayonnaise in a mixing bowl and stir until thoroughly combined.

Lay out each wrap. Halve the avocado, then remove the seed and the skin. Cut each half into slices. Divide the slices equally between the wraps.

Divide the tuna salad equally between the wraps. Roll up and serve.

4.5 ounces high quality tuna packed in olive oil, drained

¼ cup finely chopped celery

1 tablespoon finely chopped fresh flat leaf parsley

⅛ teaspoon lemon zest

Pinch of finely ground black pepper

¼ cup mayonnaise, or plain whole Greek yogurt

2 large wraps (gluten free: substitute large gluten free wraps or large tortillas)

1 avocado

Salmon with Dill Honey Mustard Sauce

Why You'll Love It:
The quintessential pairing of salmon and dill gets even better when fresh dill is incorporated into a creamy sauce with a honey mustard twist.

Prep Time: 5 minutes | Cook Time: 12 minutes | Total Time: 17 minutes | Yield: 4 servings

For the salmon:

Position an oven rack 6 inches from the broiler element. Preheat the oven on the broil setting.

Place salmon on a baking sheet. Juice the lemon over the salmon until the salmon is evenly coated with lemon juice. Brush olive oil on salmon. Top with sea salt and oregano.

Broil for 10 to 12 minutes.

For the sauce:

De-stem the dill by gripping the tip of a frond with one hand, then slide the thumb and forefinger of your other hand against the direction of growth to remove the dill leaves. You'll need about ¼ cup of dill leaves.

Mix together the dill, mayonnaise, honey mustard, and water. Top the cooked salmon with the dill honey mustard sauce.

For the salmon:

1 pound salmon

1 lemon

1 tablespoon olive oil

1 teaspoon dried oregano

¼ teaspoon sea salt

For the sauce:

1 bunch dill

½ cup mayonnaise

¼ cup honey mustard

1 tablespoon water

Recipe contributed by Melissa Eboli, also known as Chef Via Melissa, a certified Culinary Nutrition Expert (CNE), Nutritional Chef and wellness counselor based out of NY.

Lemon Pepper Cod

Why You'll Love It:
With just a few ingredients, this dinner recipe is the very definition of simplicity. A quick saltwater brine gives the cod fillets just the right amount of saltiness while also helping to prevent any white protein from appearing during the cooking process.

Prep Time: 10 minutes | Cook Time: 10 minutes | Total Time: 20 minutes | Yield: 4 servings

Cut the lemon into 4 equal wedges and set aside. Combine 2 tablespoons of salt with 2 cups of water and submerge the cod fillets for 10 minutes, then pat dry.

Add 2 tablespoons of extra virgin olive oil to a large nonstick skillet and swirl to coat. Brush the cod fillets on all sides with a light coating of extra virgin olive oil. Heat the skillet over medium heat until hot; a drop of water added to the skillet should quickly and audibly sizzle away.

Place the cod fillets in the pan with space in between them. Cook on one side for about 5 minutes, then flip each fillet and cook for about 5 minutes more (exact timing will depend on how thick the fillet is), or until the fish is opaque and flakes easily with a fork. Use a clean turner to remove the cod fillets to plates.

Season the finished cod fillets with freshly ground pepper and a generous squeeze of lemon juice from a lemon wedge.

1 lemon

2 tablespoons salt (for the brine)

4 cod fillets, equal to about 1 pound of cod

2 tablespoons extra virgin olive oil for the pan, plus a little extra for brushing the cod

Freshly ground black pepper

Vegetarian

Black Rice with Butternut Squash

Why You'll Love It:
Sweetness, savoriness, and nuttiness combine in each forkful of this comforting vegetarian rice bowl. Black rice provides glorious color and extra nutrients.

Prep Time: 35 minutes | Cook Time: 45 minutes | Total Time: 1 hour 20 minutes | Yield: 4 servings

For the rice and butternut squash:

Preheat oven to 375°F.

Cook rice according to package instructions. Drain if needed, and place in a large bowl to cool to room temperature.

While the rice is cooking, peel and seed squash and cut into bite-sized cubes. Place cubes on a large rimmed baking sheet.

Slice onion and cut slices into 1-inch pieces. Place onions on the baking sheet with the squash.

Sprinkle cumin, ginger, salt, and pepper over the squash and onions.

Drizzle olive oil on top and toss to coat. Spread out squash and onions in a single layer.

Roast until squash is tender, about 30 minutes. Allow to cool to room temperature.

Toast walnuts by spreading them on another baking sheet and bake until fragrant, about 6 to 8 minutes.

Add squash, onions, walnuts, and parsley to the bowl with the rice.

Pour dressing on top and gently toss to combine. Taste and adjust seasoning with salt and pepper.

For the dressing:

Whisk together oil, vinegar, and maple syrup in a small bowl.

For the rice and butternut squash:

1 cup uncooked black rice

1 small butternut squash

1 small red onion

¾ teaspoon ground cumin

½ teaspoon ground ginger

½ teaspoon salt

¼ teaspoon fresh ground pepper

1 tablespoon olive oil

½ cup chopped walnuts

2 tablespoons chopped fresh parsley

For the dressing:

3 tablespoons olive oil

2 tablespoons sherry vinegar

2 teaspoons maple syrup

Rigatoni with Arugula Pistou

Why You'll Love It:
This pasta dish is sauced with a variation on pistou, which is a French version of pesto, which gives it a lovely green color and a robust herbal flavor.

Prep Time: 15 minutes | Cook Time: 20 minutes | Total Time: 35 minutes | Yield: 4 servings

For the pistou:

Fill a mixing bowl halfway with ice and add enough water to cover the ice. Fill a large pot halfway with water and bring to a boil. Plunge the arugula and basil into the boiling water, stirring as needed to submerge evenly. Boil for 20 seconds, then remove arugula and basil with a slotted spoon and place it in the ice water.

Swirl the ice water to chill the arugula and basil quickly. Remove the arugula and basil from the ice water, squeezing out as much water as possible. You can form the arugula and basil into a ball and squeeze it with paper towels to remove even more water.

Place the arugula and basil with the rest of the pistou ingredients in a blender or food processor and process until smooth.

For the pasta:

Cook the pasta in salted boiling water according to the cooking directions on the package.

While the pasta is cooking, heat olive oil in a pan over medium heat and add the mushrooms and asparagus. Season with a pinch of salt and pepper. Cook for 5 to 10 minutes, or until the mushrooms are nicely browned (caramelized) and the asparagus is tender.

When the pasta is almost ready, add all of the pistou to the vegetables in the pan and stir to coat. Drain the pasta, then add the drained pasta to the pan. Toss the pasta to incorporate the ingredients, then taste and adjust seasoning by adding more salt and pepper if needed.

Divide into four servings. Divide the bread crumbs, parmesan cheese, and lemon zest equally as a garnish to each serving. Serve immediately.

Recipe contributed by The Little Beet Table, a convivial all-day restaurant that serves nourishing and gluten-free food without a hint of pretentiousness.

For the pistou:

5 cups arugula, lightly packed (about 5 ounces)

1 cup fresh basil leaves, lightly packed (about ½ ounce)

1 garlic clove, peeled

¼ teaspoon chopped fresh jalapeno pepper

½ cup olive oil

¼ teaspoon salt

For the pasta:

8 ounces rigatoni (gluten free: substitute any gluten free pasta)

1 teaspoon olive oil

2 cups mixed mushrooms (about 4 ounces)

1 cup asparagus cut into 1 inch pieces (about 4 ounces)

Salt

Pepper

2 tablespoons bread crumbs (gluten free: substitute seasoned gluten free bread crumbs)

2 tablespoons grated parmesan cheese

Zest of 1 lemon

Sheet Pan Tahini Roasted Vegetables

Why You'll Love It:
You can make as many variations of this recipe as you can imagine. It works equally well with a variety of vegetables, such butternut squash and onions, or Brussels sprouts and sweet potatoes.

Prep Time: 10 minutes | Cook Time: 30 minutes | Total Time: 40 minutes | Yield: 2 to 4 servings

---

Preheat the oven to 400°F.

Wash and chop the broccoli and cauliflower into small florets. Dry the vegetables and place in a bowl. Lightly drizzle the olive oil over the vegetables and coat evenly. Season with salt and pepper.

Evenly place vegetables on a baking sheet and roast for about 30 minutes. Take vegetables out when they are browned, with a slight crunch.

At the same time, but on a separate baking sheet, roast the chickpeas until they get crunchy and start to dry out, around 15 minutes.

In a small blender, combine the ingredients for the tahini sauce and adjust the flavoring and consistency.

When the roasted vegetables and chickpeas are done, place everything into a bowl and pour in the tahini sauce to coast everything evenly. Season with additional salt and pepper if desired.

Recipe contributed by Wade Brill, a Professional Certified Life Coach, Energy Leadership Index Practitioner, as well as a Mindfulness Facilitator through UCLA's Semel Institute for Neuroscience and Human Behavior.

Whole broccoli head

Whole cauliflower head

2 cups cooked chickpeas (canned chickpeas work fine)

2 tablespoons extra virgin olive oil

Salt (Himalayan pink salt recommended)

Pepper

For the tahini sauce:

¼ cup tahini paste

2 tablespoons soy sauce or Bragg Liquid Aminos (gluten free: use Bragg Liquid Aminos or substitute gluten free soy sauce)

3 tablespoons freshly squeezed lemon juice

2 garlic cloves, minced

3 tablespoons water (add more for thinner sauce consistency)

Liquid Aminos

KNOW YOUR INGREDIENTS

Similar to soy sauce and tamari sauce, liquid aminos add a powerful punch of savory or "umami" flavoring. They can be made from soybeans or from coconut tree sap. Liquid aminos are typically gluten free and, unlike soy sauce, can be a dietary source of amino acids.

Soy-based liquid aminos taste similar to soy sauce, but milder and with less sodium. Coconut aminos are also similar in flavor to soy sauce, but have a slightly sweeter flavor profile and contain even less sodium. Keep in mind that even though liquid aminos can be lower in sodium than soy sauce, they still contain a significant amount of sodium. You can substitute liquid aminos equally for soy sauce in a recipe.

Broccoli Cheese Soup

Why You'll Love It:
This delectably cheesy soup is a good way to eat your veggies in the most appetizing way possible.

Prep Time: 5 minutes | Cook Time: 15 minutes | Total Time: 20 minutes | Yield: 4 servings

Combine the half-and-half with the chicken stock in a pitcher or container with a spout for pouring. Set aside for the moment.

In a pot, melt the butter over low to medium heat. Whisk the flour into the melted butter. Continue whisking and cooking the flour and butter paste until it turns a light tan color.

Whisk in the liquid (the mixture of half-and-half with stock) a little bit at a time, each time whisking until smooth before adding more liquid. After all the liquid has been incorporated, continue cooking and whisking for several minutes to make it very smooth, but do not let it boil.

Add nutmeg and salt and pepper to taste. Add the cooked broccoli. Stir well.

Add shredded cheese ½ cup at a time, stirring after each addition until completely smooth and fully incorporated. Taste the soup and add salt and pepper, a pinch at a time, if needed.

- 2 cups half-and-half
- 2 cups vegetable stock
- ¼ cup butter
- ¼ cup flour (gluten free: substitute gluten free baking flour mix)
- 8 ounces shredded cheddar
- 2 cups cooked broccoli
- Pinch of nutmeg
- Salt
- Pepper

Toasty Bagel Sandwiches

Why You'll Love It:
Loaded with fresh vegetables, satisfying hummus, rich avocado slices, and two kinds of cheese, these toasty bagel sandwiches demonstrate that you don't need meat to make a fantastic sandwich.

Prep Time: 5 minutes | Cook Time: 5 minutes | Total Time: 10 minutes | Yield: 4 bagel sandwiches

Begin preheating the oven to 400°F. Toast the bagels in a toaster. Place 4 of the bagel halves on a baking sheet, cut side up. Top each with a slice of pepper jack cheese. Place in heated oven for 5 minutes.

While the cheese is melting on the bagel halves in the oven, divide the hummus equally between the remaining bagel halves. Top each equally with goat cheese crumbles followed by arugula, then avocado slices, then a tomato slice.

Remove the bagel halves from the oven. Top each bagel sandwich bottom half with a melted cheese top half and serve immediately.

4 bagels, split (gluten free: substitute gluten free bagels, English muffins, or bread)

4 slices pepper jack cheese

1 cup hummus

¼ cup goat cheese crumbles

2 avocados, seeds removed, peeled and sliced

1 cup arugula

4 tomato slices

Cilantro Pesto Black Bean Burgers

Why You'll Love It:
There's better flavor in these homemade black bean burgers than you'll ever find in the prepackaged kind. A topping of tangy pesto sauce and avocado slices adds just the right amount of coolness to balance the spice in the burgers.

Prep Time: 10 minutes | Inactive Time: 1 hour | Cook Time: 20 minutes
Total Time: 1 hour 30 minutes | Yield: 4 servings

To create the burgers, mash black beans in a medium bowl until you have created a thick paste.

Finely chop onion, garlic, cilantro, green chilies, and chopped red pepper, then mix into the mashed black bean paste.

Add chili powder, cumin, egg whites, and bread crumbs, then mix until the mixture is combined and holds together.

Form mixture into four equal sized patties. Place patties on a baking sheet lined with parchment paper. Refrigerate patties for one hour.

Heat grill or skillet to medium heat. Cook patties over medium heat for 8 to 10 minutes per side.

To create pesto sauce, combine the cilantro, pumpkin seeds, garlic, fresh lime juice, and salt in a food processor, then pulse ingredients until coarsely chopped. With the processor running, slowly add olive oil through the feed tube. Add yogurt and blend until well mixed.

Serve burgers topped with sliced avocado and creamy cilantro pesto sauce.

Special Equipment: Food processor

For the black bean burgers:

1 (16 ounce) can black beans, drained and rinsed

½ red bell pepper

½ onion

1 clove garlic, peeled and crushed

2 tablespoons green chilies

¼ cup fresh cilantro leaves

2 egg whites

1 teaspoon chili powder

1 teaspoon cumin

⅔ cup bread crumbs (gluten free: use gluten free bread crumbs)

1 avocado, sliced

For the pesto sauce:

2 cups fresh cilantro leaves

⅓ cup unsalted pumpkin seeds

1 clove garlic

2 tablespoons fresh lime juice

½ teaspoon salt

2 tablespoons olive oil

¼ cup nonfat plain Greek yogurt

Recipe contributed by Jimmy Slagle, Kitchen Conquered Host, sixteen-time bestselling author, Harvard Educated Fine Dining Experimentalist, and 7-Figure Entrepreneur.

Tarragon Goat Cheese Egg Salad Sandwiches

Why You'll Love It:
These protein-packed egg salad sandwiches are elevated with a touch of fresh tarragon and a handful of piquant goat cheese crumbles. If you keep hard-boiled eggs on hand, you'll always be ready to whip these up in a jiffy.

Prep Time: 10 minutes | Cook Time: 20 minutes | Inactive Time: 1 hour
Total Time: 1 hour 30 minutes | Yield: 4 sandwiches

Place eggs in a single layer in a saucepan and cover with 1 inch of water. Add ¼ teaspoon salt. Bring to a boil. Cover and remove from heat.

Let stand for 15 minutes. Drain water and replace with cold water and ice. Let eggs cool for 5 minutes.

Peel eggs. After you peel each egg, lightly rinse it to make sure you remove all shell bits. Then place the egg on paper towels.

Place eggs in a medium bowl. Use a fork to mash and crumble the eggs.

Add goat cheese, tarragon, salt, and pepper. Stir to combine.

Fold in mayonnaise. Cover and chill for at least 1 hour.

Top 4 slices of bread with lettuce, tomato, and egg salad. Cover with remaining slices of bread.

6 large eggs

3 ounces goat cheese crumbles

1 teaspoon finely chopped fresh tarragon leaves

¼ teaspoon salt

⅛ teaspoon pepper

6 tablespoons mayonnaise

8 slices bread, toasted (gluten free: substitute gluten free sandwich bread)

2 cups lettuce leaves (green leaf or romaine)

2 tomatoes, sliced

Creamy Potato Soup

Why You'll Love It:
Who can resist a creamy soup? This potato soup can be enjoyed in all its smooth simplicity, or it can be a canvas for your favorite soup toppings like shredded cheese and crunchy croutons.

Prep Time: 15 minutes | Cook Time: 30 minutes | Total Time: 45 minutes | Yield: 4 to 6 servings

Place potatoes in a medium saucepan. Add enough water to just cover potatoes. Add green onions, celery, salt, and pepper.

Bring to a boil, then reduce heat to medium. Cover loosely and cook until potatoes are cooked through and tender, about 20 minutes.

Add milk, half-and-half, and butter. Stir and cook until butter melts.

Purée with an immersion blender or in a regular blender. Garnish with additional sliced green onion if desired.

Special Equipment: Immersion blender or regular blender

6 medium russet potatoes, peeled and cut into small cubes

2 cups water, plus more if needed

4 green onions, white and light green part only, sliced

1 celery stalk, diced

2 teaspoons salt

½ teaspoon ground white pepper

2 cups whole milk

1 cup half-and-half

½ cup unsalted butter

Grilled Pimento Cheese Sandwiches

Why You'll Love It:
Made from a mixture of four cheeses and studded with brightly colored pimentos, these sandwiches will become your new comfort food indulgence.

Prep Time: 10 minutes | Inactive Time: 3 hours | Cook Time: 5 minutes
Total Time: 3 hours 15 minutes | Yield: 4 cups pimento cheese, enough for 6 sandwiches

---

In the bowl of a food processor fitted with a knife blade, process cream cheese, mayonnaise, onion, garlic powder, salt, and pepper until smooth.

Add the shredded cheeses and pimentos and pulse to combine. Do not over-process. Transfer pimento cheese to a bowl and stir if needed to combine ingredients thoroughly. Cover and chill for at least 3 hours.

Heat a skillet or griddle to medium heat. Do not get too hot or it will burn the butter and bread.

Butter one side of two bread slices. Spread a thick layer of pimento cheese on the un-buttered side of a bread slice.

Place pimento cheese covered bread slice butter side down in the skillet. Cover skillet with a lid and cook for 1 minute.

Remove lid and top sandwich with the other slice butter side up. Cook until bottom is lightly browned and toasted.

Flip sandwich over and cook until the other side is lightly browned and toasted.

Transfer sandwich to a plate and slice in half.

Repeat with remaining bread and pimento cheese or grill 2 to 4 sandwiches at a time, depending on size of skillet. Do not over-crowd the skillet.

Refrigerate extra pimento cheese for up to 5 days.

Special Equipment: Food processor

¼ cup cream cheese, at room temperature

3 tablespoons mayonnaise

⅛ teaspoon garlic powder

Pinch of salt

Pinch of fresh ground pepper

2 cups shredded sharp cheddar cheese

1 cup shredded pepper jack cheese

1 cup shredded Monterey Jack cheese

4 ounce jar chopped pimentos, drained

Slices of hearty white bread (gluten free: substitute gluten free sandwich bread)

Butter, softened for easy spreading

On The Side

ON THE SIDE

How to Roast Almost Any Vegetable

Roasting vegetables brings out their natural sweetness. All you need is a little salt, a little olive oil, and a baking sheet. If you have parchment paper, you can line your baking sheet with it for easy cleanup.

Here are a few favorites to try: acorn squash, butternut squash, asparagus, bell peppers, broccoli, Brussels sprouts, carrots, cauliflower, green beans, yellow squash, zucchini.

The most important thing to remember is that vegetables roasted at the same time should be approximately the same size and density. A mixture of cut yellow squash and zucchini is an example of this. Yellow squash and zucchini can be cut into similar sized pieces and will cook at the same rate, where as a combination of butternut squash (very dense) and bell peppers (not dense) would overcook the bell peppers long before the butternut squash was done. You can stick to single vegetables until you get the hang of roasting. Later, you can get adventurous with combinations.

Although you can roast vegetables at a variety of temperatures, 400°F is a safe bet that works for just about anything without risking scorching the vegetables before they are fully cooked. It's a great way to get fork-tender texture with delicious browning around the edges.

Toss your evenly-sized vegetables in enough olive oil to give them a very light coating of oil. They should not look like they've been drenched in oil. Start with a little and add more if needed.

After the vegetables have been lightly oiled, sprinkle on a little bit of salt, then toss to distribute the salt. Add a little more salt and toss again. Arrange the vegetables on the baking sheet, not touching or just barely touching each other.

Place the baking sheet in the preheated oven and roast the vegetables until a fork pierces them easily. The amount of time will vary depending on the vegetable. Delicate vegetables like asparagus will roast quickly, in 15 to 20 minutes, whereas larger or denser vegetables may take 30 to 45 minutes. To determine doneness, vegetables should be tender enough to be easily pierced with a fork, at least slightly brown, and a bit crispy around the edges.

For an extra treat, garnish with freshly grated parmesan cheese before serving.

ON THE SIDE
Baked Potatoes

To make baked potatoes, preheat the oven to 400°F. Rinse and scrub the potatoes thoroughly. Prick them a few times with a fork. Sprinkle salt over the wet skin. Place the potatoes on a baking sheet and bake for 1 hour, or until done. Split them open immediately (watch out, they're hot!), gently squeeze both ends toward each other to fluff up the inside, then serve with your favorite toppings.

- *Alfredo*: chopped or pulled chicken, Alfredo sauce, chopped fresh parsley, parmesan
- *Classic*: cheddar, sour cream, bacon, chives
- *Cheeseburger*: crumbled ground beef or burger patty, cheese, pickles, condiments
- *BBQ*: pulled pork or chicken, barbecue sauce, coleslaw
- *BLT*: bacon, chopped tomato, ranch dressing, chopped lettuce
- *Breakfast*: scrambled eggs, breakfast sausage, hot sauce
- *Broccoli Cheddar*: chopped cooked broccoli, cheddar cheese (and/or thick broccoli cheese soup)
- *Buffalo*: pulled chicken, Buffalo wing sauce, blue cheese or ranch dressing, chopped celery
- *Italian*: ricotta cheese, chopped sundried tomatoes in oil, freshly ground black pepper
- *Mediterranean*: hummus, olives, chopped tomato, crumbled feta cheese
- *Pizza*: pepperoni, melted mozzarella, tomato sauce
- *Roast Beef*: sliced roast beef, horseradish sauce, cheddar
- *Sausage & Peppers*: cooked sausage and bell peppers
- *Taco*: seasoned black beans, Mexican cheese, avocado, sour cream, salsa, cilantro
- *Thanksgiving*: gravy, sliced turkey, cranberry sauce

ON THE SIDE

Salads

These salads will round off any dinner. Try a lighter salad with a rich dinner, like a wedge salad alongside a roast; pair a protein-rich salad with a light dinner, like a chef salad with broccoli cheese soup. Vary or omit ingredients to suit your taste.

- *Antipasto:* chopped lettuce, sliced Italian meats (such as Parma ham, capocollo, or prosciutto), buffalo mozzarella torn into bite sized pieces, chopped jarred artichokes and sun-dried tomatoes, red wine vinaigrette
- *Caprese*: sliced fresh mozzarella, sliced tomatoes, fresh basil, balsamic vinegar
- *Cobb*: chopped lettuce, chopped chicken, chopped hard boiled egg, chopped tomatoes, chopped bacon, blue cheese crumbles, sliced avocado, red wine vinaigrette
- *Coleslaw*: shredded cabbage or coleslaw mix; make a sauce to coat by combining mayonnaise plus a touch of apple cider vinegar and honey to taste
- *Chef*: chopped lettuce, julienned deli meat (such as ham and/or turkey), sliced hard boiled egg, cubed cheddar cheese, sliced cucumber, chopped tomato
- *Chinese*: chopped lettuce, shredded cabbage, chopped chicken, mandarin oranges, slivered almonds, Asian sesame dressing, chow mein noodles (gluten free: omit these)
- *Greek*: chopped lettuce, chopped tomatoes, olives, sliced cucumber, thinly sliced red onion, crumbled feta cheese, Greek or red wine vinaigrette
- *Niçoise*: chopped lettuce, quartered tomatoes, high quality canned tuna, anchovies, and black olives, dressed with olive oil and salt to taste
- *Spinach*: fresh baby spinach, dried cranberries, chopped pecans, crumbled goat cheese, honey mustard dressing
- *Taco*: chopped lettuce, cooked ground beef seasoned with chili powder, shredded Mexican cheese, chopped tomatoes, sliced avocado, seasoned black beans, corn, sour cream, cilantro, and tortilla chips or broken taco shells
- *Waldorf*: chopped apples, chopped celery, chopped walnuts, and halved grapes mixed with a little mayonnaise until coated, then served on a bed of lettuce
- *Wedge*: chilled wedges of iceberg lettuce topped with ranch dressing, crumbled bacon, pepitas, finely chopped tomatoes, and croutons (gluten free: substitute gluten free croutons or parmesan crisps)

RECIPE INDEX

Amalfi Coast Risotto 45

Apple Cranberry Pecan Chicken Salad 37

Bacon and Blue Cheese Pasta with Grilled Steak 3

Baked Cavatini 8

Basil Buttered Shrimp with Vegetables 52

Bison Meatloaf 13

Black Rice with Butternut Squash 62

Boliche (Cuban Stuffed Roast) 17

Broccoli Cheese Soup 66

Buffalo Chicken Quesadillas 36

Cedar Plank Salmon 44

Chili Cheese Potato Parfait 15

Cilantro Pesto Black Bean Burgers 68

Citrus Chimichurri Shrimp Rice 46

Corn and Andouille Sausage Chowder 30

Creamy Potato Soup 70

Gnocchi with Italian Sausage 25

Greek Meatball Salad 10

Grilled Chicken Caesar Salad 40

Grilled Pimento Cheese Sandwiches 71

Irish Bacon and Cheese Frittata 28

Latkes with Smoked Salmon 55

Lemon Pepper Cod 58

Meatza 4

Mushroom and Swiss Stuffed Turkey Burgers 34

New York Strip Roast 11

One Pan Roasted Asian Pork and Vegetables 22

Pork Chops and Sauerkraut 23

Pulled Pork in the Oven 26

Quick Spaghetti and Meatballs 14

Red Wine Pot Roast 2
Rigatoni with Arugula Pistou 63
Roast Pork Loin Filet with Whole Mushrooms 27
Salmon with Dill Honey Mustard Sauce 57
Sheet Pan Tahini Roasted Vegetables 64
Sherry Apple Pork Roast 31
Smash Burgers 16
Spicy Shrimp Tacos 53
Spinach Cream Cheese Stuffed Chicken Breast Wrapped in Bacon 38
Steak and Egg Bowl 6
Tarragon Goat Cheese Egg Salad Sandwiches 69
Tater Tot Hotdish 5
Thai Shrimp Curry 49
Toasty Bagel Sandwiches 67
Tortilla Chip Crusted Turkey Cutlets 41
Tuna Cakes 50
Tuna Salad Wraps 56
Turkey Reuben Panini 39
Vietnamese Banh Mi Bowls 7
Yogurt Marinated Chicken 35

KNOW YOUR INGREDIENTS INDEX

Bacon 29
Bison 12
Canned Tuna 51
Chorizo ....
Gnocchi 24
Liquid aminos 65
Mozzarella 9
Rice 47
Shrimp 48
Smoked Salmon 54

Contributors

Wade Brill is a Professional Certified Life Coach, Energy Leadership Index Practitioner, as well as a Mindfulness Facilitator through UCLA's Semel Institute for Neuroscience and Human Behavior. A firm believer that when you feel good from the inside out, you can do good for the world, Wade supports individuals and companies around the country, practicing self-care so that they can prevent burnout and instead be more present and productive in life. As a cancer survivor and thriver, Wade embodies the rule: self-care isn't selfish, it's smart.

Renee Dobbs is a self-proclaimed Domestic Goddess who loves to eat, drink, and dig in the dirt. She is enjoying life in the South and experiencing flavors from around the world. Cooking will always be one of her passions along with gardening and spoiling her whippets. You can read more of her food adventures on Magnolia Days, a blog she created and filled with recipes until retiring from it in 2017.

Melissa Eboli also known as Chef Via Melissa is a certified Culinary Nutrition Expert (CNE), Nutritional Chef and wellness counselor based out of NY. She is the author of "The Anti-Anxiety Recipe Plan" (2019), and the owner of Via's Kitchen, a personal chef and catering company that focuses on clean, allergen friendly food. Her services include event catering, dinner parties, cooking classes and recipe development. When she's not in the kitchen, she can be seen making guest appearances on Dr.Oz, in addition to being published in the likes of The New York Times, Forbes and Readers Digest. Her passion as a chef is to create healthy dishes with a modern twist using the cleanest of ingredients while focusing on nutrition, flavor and presentation.

Sherri Hagymas is the author of *To Simply Inspire*. She lives in New Hampshire with her husband, 2 kids and fur baby, Teddy. When she is not cooking or updating her older home, you can find her in the gym or enjoying the outdoors.

Luisa Ruocco is a London based Italian-British social media food and travel influencer who spends her summers on the Amalfi Coast. She grows her own lemons which she loves using to make limoncello or her citrusy risotto. You can follow her culinary adventures on Instagram @luisainsta.

Caitlin Self (MS, CNS, LDN) is a lifelong food lover, nutritionist, and blogger. She has been developing recipes for both internet readers and clients in real life since 2012. She is the licensed nutritionist behind www.frugalnutrition.com and www.caitlinselfnutrition.com and especially loves gluten-free, dairy-free, and Paleo-style meals and baked goods. Follow her for more recipes and nutrition tips on Instagram @frugalnutrition.

Jimmy Slagle is a Kitchen Conquered Host, sixteen-time bestselling author, Harvard Educated Fine Dining Experimentalist, and 7-Figure Entrepreneur. He is the founder of CulinaryOrgasms.agency, a specialty marketing and public relations firm that helps entrepreneurial chefs become iconic in their craft; Musicians Menu: What happens when you bring world class chefs together with world class musicians? A seven course dinner and live concert experience unlike anything you've ever seen, heard, or tasted; Chef Table VIP: Offering exclusive tasting menu and chef table experiences for any occasion; and Kitchen Conquered: Where world-class celebrity chefs reveal their proven techniques, strategies, skills, and tools to help home cooks prepare, audition, and compete on their favorite reality cooking show.

The Little Beet Table is a convivial all-day restaurant that serves nourishing and gluten-free food without a hint of pretentiousness. Dedicated to fostering community and providing a haven for guests with a variety of dietary preferences, the eatery offers intuitive and thoughtful service, always evolving to better serve its guests. The LBT menu consists of vegetable-forward plates, comfort food classics, housemade juices, and vegetable-centric cocktails that ably walk the line between wholesome and indulgent.

Recommended Reading

I Hate Vegetables Cookbook: Fresh and Easy Vegetable Recipes That Will Change Your Mind is the perfect companion to the *I Love Dinner Cookbook*.

Think you're a veggie hater who could never enjoy vegetables? Do salads make you wilt? Do sprouts make you shudder? Then this is the cookbook for you! With the help of the I Hate Vegetables Cookbook, you'll learn to love vegetables one great recipe at a time. Say goodbye to overcooked and under-seasoned vegetables. Learn to enhance them with flavor-boosting cooking methods and complementary ingredients.

Get every recipe right the first time with easy-to-follow instructions, explanations of lesser-known ingredients, and handy tips from pro chefs.

Become a veggie lover, not a veggie hater, with loads of delicious dishes like Buffalo Style Oven Roasted Cauliflower, Smoky Sweet Potato Soup, and Maple Butter Roasted Squash. Savor amazing salads like Sugar Snap Pea Salad with Prosciutto, Parmigiano, and Sherry Vinaigrette. Indulge in comfort food classics like Garlic Cheddar Biscuit-Topped Vegetable Pot Pie. Plus, every recipe can be made gluten free and vegetarian.

Buy it on Amazon today!

Katie Moseman

ABOUT THE AUTHOR

Katie Moseman is a cookbook author, food photographer, and recipe developer whose work can be found on her blogs, Recipe for Perfection and Magnolia Days, as well as in numerous national publications. She lives in Florida with her family.

www.ingramcontent.com/pod-product-compliance
Lightning Source LLC
Chambersburg PA
CBHW060426010526
44118CB00017B/2378